MW00991010

Rational Investing

Rational Investing

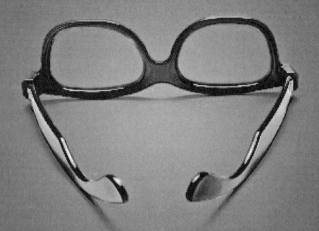

The **SUBTLETIES** of **ASSET MANAGEMENT**

Hugues Langlois and
Jacques Lussier

Columbia Business School
Publishing

Columbia University Press
Publishers Since 1893
New York   Chichester, West Sussex
cup.columbia.edu

Copyright © 2017 Columbia University Press
All rights reserved

Library of Congress Cataloging-in-Publication Data
Names: Langlois, Hugues, 1983– author. |
Lussier, Jacques (Investment Strategist), author.
Title: Rational investing : the subtleties of asset management /
Hugues Langlois and Jacques Lussier.
Description: New York : Columbia University Press, [2016] |
Includes bibliographical references and index.
Identifiers: LCCN 2016039622 | ISBN 9780231177344 (cloth : alk. paper)
Subjects: LCSH: Portfolio management. | Investments.
Classification: LCC HG4529.5 .L87 2016 | DDC 332.6—dc23
LC record available at https://lccn.loc.gov/2016039622

Columbia University Press books are printed on permanent
and durable acid-free paper.
Printed in the United States of America

Cover design: Noah Arlow

Contents

Contents

Rational Investing

I

The Subtleties of Asset Management

THIS BOOK IS ABOUT bridging the gap between simplicity and complexity in asset management. It is about providing nonprofessional investors with an understanding of what underlies investment success while still making investment professionals reflect on many issues they may have forgotten or overlooked. It is about achieving these objectives in fewer than two hundred pages because the essence and clarity of a message are often lost in the thickness or the specialization of the medium of communication. And it is a tremendous challenge.

It is a challenge because asset management is an industry in which conflicts of interest are omnipresent, and the conversation is often adjusted to protect the interests of some of the players. In the last twenty years, the asset management industry has not only developed better investment strategies, but unfortunately also ways to package existing investment products and repackage old ideas, often at a higher cost. You may have already heard of the separation of alpha and beta; alpha overlay or transport; alternative, exotic, and now smart beta; fundamental indexing; core versus satellite components; liability-driven investment (LDI); performance-seeking portfolios (PSP); etc. It is a challenge to succinctly present a framework for understanding all of these concepts while each is often improperly pushed as a distinctive breakthrough. It is nonetheless the objective of this book.

It is also a challenge because asset management is not just about financial concepts. It is also about economics more generally, mathematics, statistics, psychology, history, and sociology. A comprehensive investment approach requires a comprehensive understanding of all these fields, a knowledge base few of us have. Investors' education is therefore both essential and difficult. Building a lasting cumulative body of knowledge requires drawing evidence from many different literatures. The objective of this book is to provide the broadest possible understanding of the factors that drive investment successes and failures while avoiding as much as possible the complexity, biases, and noise that surround it.

For example, in disciplines such as astronomy and physics, we build our body of knowledge through relevant experimentation that hopefully allows for consensus among experts. This process provides a foundation for furthering our understanding through new research. Few physicists would challenge the idea that a body with more mass exerts greater gravity. In contrast, most investors and professional managers believe they are above average. More generally, the interaction between investment research and the financial markets it studies results in a constant evolution of these markets. The complexity of asset management and its interaction with social sciences also implies that it is difficult to build a clear consensus. It is therefore possible for players in that industry to simply ignore empirical evidence and rational thinking if it challenges the viability of existing business models. This is implicitly reflected in the answer given by Jeremy Grantham of GMO when he was asked about what would be learned from the turmoil of 2008: "We will learn an enormous amount in the very short term, quite a bit in the medium term, and absolutely nothing in the long term. That would be the historical precedent."[1]

Given these complexities, it is not surprising to see that there is a significant divide between the enormous body of literature developed by financial academicians and the body of research and practices accumulated by practitioners. Once we integrate knowledge from different areas of literature and work hard at making our thinking clean and simple, it becomes easier to explain the sources of success in terms that most investors can understand.

The main objective of this book is to explain all structural sources of performance and to illustrate their implementation. To this end, we cover many topics. We will discuss that there are talented and skilled professional fund managers out there, but that unfortunately not a lot of the value they create ends up in investors' pockets. We will show that forecasting expected returns is not a useless endeavor, but it is usually not the primary source of sustainable excess performance of successful managers despite the rhetoric.

This book was written with the objective of communicating what is required to invest rationally while making its content accessible to as wide an audience as possible. It avoids the overuse of equations and of complex terminologies. In fact, we have managed to write this entire book with just a few equations. The length limitation we imposed on ourselves also dictates that we concentrate on the most relevant concepts and evidence.

The framework used in this book is not revolutionary, nor do we need it to be. We are not reinventing the wheel. We are presenting an overall picture of asset management through which we are going to underline many subtleties of this fascinating field that can allow us to sustainably outperform others. Investing in financial markets is a lottery only if we do not understand what drives long-term performance.

What This Book Is Not About

This book is *not* about saying that markets are perfectly efficient or inefficient. Market efficiency says that all the information relevant to the valuation of an investment is reflected in its price. If the price of any asset perfectly reflected its true fundamental value, there would be no point in spending resources trying to spot good investment opportunities to beat the market. Whatever you buy, you get a fair price for the risk you are getting into. But market inefficiency proponents point out that investors are not perfectly rational investing robots. They are influenced by their emotions and behavioral biases, and as a result asset prices can differ from their fundamental values in such a way that riskless profits can be made. Hence an investor could beat the market by looking for good investment opportunities.

It can't be that easy; prices cannot be completely irrational and erratic. Many smart investors compete with each other to profit from potential market inefficiencies, and few are able to make a killing at it. The reality lies in between. Markets have to be inefficient enough to make it worthwhile for investors to spend time and resources analyzing different investments and looking for good opportunities. But they cannot be so inefficient that it is easy to beat the market. If undervalued securities could be spotted easily, all investors could buy them and push up their prices to a fair level. A similar argument applies to overvalued securities. To borrow the characterization from Lasse Pedersen, professor of finance at New York University Stern School of Business and Copenhagen Business School, markets are *efficiently inefficient.*[2] This book discusses sources of investment profits coming from both sides: rational compensations for the risks supported by investors and irrationalities in financial markets caused by emotions and other behavioral aspects.

On a related note, this book is *not* about taking sides in the debate between passive and active management. Passive managers simply invest in the market index, that is, a portfolio that includes all assets whose allocations depend on their market capitalization (i.e., their market value), such as buying the S&P 500 Index. Active managers look for good investments and try to beat the market index. Widespread evidence shows that most active managers fail to outperform the market index, and since the first index fund was launched in the 1970s, passive investments have gained in popularity. Exchange traded funds (ETF) now offer the possibility for investors to invest in a wide variety of market indexes at a low cost. Who is right? Again, the reality lies in between. There are talented investors out there and we all have a lot to learn from them. The important issue is how much of their performance actually trickles down to investors' pockets. For an active fund to be a good investment opportunity, its managers have to be good enough to cover trading costs as well as the management fees that they charge you. Accordingly, this book does not take a stance on whether you should be an active or a passive investor. Rather, it analyzes the factors that should impact your decision.

This book is *not* about diversification for the sake of diversification. Diversification is said to be the only free lunch in finance. Yet it remains an uncomfortable proposition for many investors. Aren't we buying bad investments as well as good investments when we are diversifying? Warren Buffett, famous investor and chairman of Berkshire Hathaway, said that "diversification is protection against ignorance. It makes little sense if you know what you are doing."

Diversification is often misunderstood. Diversification does not require owning thousands of stocks. A good portion of available diversification benefits can be obtained by owning a portfolio of twenty to thirty companies, similar to what Mr. Buffett does.

Nor is diversification about sacrificing returns to get lower risk; diversification can actually lead to higher long-term returns through the effect of compounding. Most importantly, diversification is not a substitute for a careful analysis of investment values. Valuation is not trumped by the power of diversification. However if you have a smart way to analyze and pick investments and you care about the level of total risk you are taking in your portfolio, there is little reason for most of us to invest in an under-diversified portfolio of just a few assets.

This book is not about any asset class (stocks, bonds, commodities, currencies, etc.) in particular. There are, of course, specificities to each market. An investment expert who spent his career trading in the government bond market knows this market better than an equity trader (and vice versa). Still, markets are not completely segmented and the investment principles discussed in this book apply broadly. Many investment styles, risk factors, and strategies work in different markets. This book focuses on building efficient portfolios in all traded asset classes using a common investment philosophy.

Finally, this book is *not* about fundamental investing versus quantitative investing. The former refers to investors who make inferences from their analyses of investment's fundamentals (cash flows, accounting value, industry trends, macroeconomic conditions, etc.). The latter can refer to investors who rely on statistical methods and computer models to pick investments, often using many of the same fundamental variables. Fundamentals are important. However, whichever emphasis you want to put on fundamentals, it is better to do it by relying on careful quantitative analysis. An investor may have the greatest intuitive skills to pick investments, but we would still prefer to confirm his analysis through careful quantitative analysis. Gut feelings are nice for movies, but very dangerous for successful long-term investing.

The Roadmap to Successful Long-Term Portfolios

To present the structure of this book, we use the framework set forth in figure 1.1. There are four distinctive blocks in the figure and one that surrounds them all.

The first box in the top left part of figure 1.1 is about the impact of market structure on performance. This is an aspect investors cannot do anything about and it is mainly the subject of chapter 2. Our discussion starts with the first decision you need to make as an investor: Should you be a passive (indexed) or an active investor? Because passive investors mimic the market portfolio, only active investors can potentially do better than the market. However, active investors as a group will do just as well as the market—no better, no worse. Indeed, active and passive investors

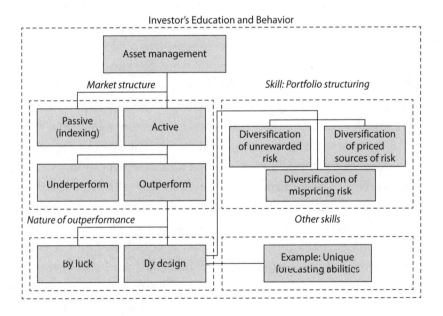

FIGURE 1.1 A schematic to asset management

are the market. In other words, if the market is up by 10 percent, passive investors will be up by 10 percent. Consequently, it goes without saying that all active investors as a group are up by 10 percent as well.

Hence an active investor can only outperform at the expense of another active investor. Some active investors will underperform while others will outperform. But if you are like us, you are not interested in simply outperforming the market. You are interested in outperforming it consistently. In this book, we want to understand what explains long-term investment successes, not short-term gains mainly due to luck.

Furthermore, to be a successful active investor over the long run, not only do you need to consistently extract value from other active investors, but you must also do it to an extent that covers the extra costs you incur by being an active manager. This is no small feat; at this point you might recognize that you do not possess such expertise. Indeed, for many investors, passive investing, with its low-cost structure, is the best deal in town. Alternatively, you may delegate the management of your portfolio to a professional fund manager. But choosing a skilled manager is far from obvious. Screening the S&P Indices Versus Active (SPIVA) scorecards, you will quickly notice that if you select an active manager at random, you likely have less than three chances out of ten of selecting a manager who will outperform after fees in the long term. The level of expertise that exists in the market does not change this observation.

Chapter 3 closely examines the difficult task of selecting a professional fund manager. The challenge here is to identify talented managers and to be able to do it in advance. Indeed, knowing which managers are good after the fact is pointless. The key issue is to distinguish genuine investing skills from pure luck. Past performance over a short horizon of a few years is often meaningless as proof of a manager's skills. Standard statistical analyses usually cannot conclude whether a manager is truly skilled after such a short period. Instead, investors must be convinced of the abilities of a manager through an understanding of his process, not by his performance over the last three years. Such confidence requires a deep understanding of relevant structural qualities within portfolios.

Chapter 4 discusses our ability to forecast complex systems such as financial markets, especially the contrast between predictions given by experts and those provided by simple statistical models. For the sake of portfolio allocations, relying on simple statistical models may lead to better forecasts because experts' forecasts can be tainted by overconfidence and conflicts of interest.

Chapters 2 to 4 are concerned with the desire to outperform the market. We cover three broad possibilities that are not mutually exclusive: being an active investor yourself (chapter 2), hiring a professional fund manager (chapter 3), and relying on forecasts to adjust your portfolio allocation (chapter 4).

The second block in the bottom left part of figure 1.1 deals with the conundrum of the role of luck versus investment skills. This is a recurring topic in several chapters of this book. Indeed, the financial market is an environment in which luck plays a large role in observed performances. By luck we mean investment performance that is due to what statisticians call *noise*, or pure randomness. Imagine a room with one thousand individuals, none of whom has any investment skill. Each individual is independently asked to determine whether he should overweight Alphabet at the expense of Amazon or the reverse for the next three years. It is likely that approximately half will be right and will outperform even if they have no investment skill. As you may imagine, we want to ensure that the success of our investment strategy does not rely on luck!

We emphasize in this book the long-term aspect of the portfolio management approaches we discuss. Luck (i.e., noise) plays a large role in short-term performance. It still plays a role in long-term performance, but to a lesser extent. To see why, imagine that you have found a strategy that is likely to generate a 10 percent return on average every year (or approximately 0.04 percent every day). But assets, such as stocks, display a lot of daily variability; it is not usual for stocks to vary between −2 percent or +2 percent every day. Hence the part of *daily* returns that you may explain on average, 0.04 percent, is hard to discern from the daily market noise. Over longer horizons, say one year, most −2 percent daily noise returns cancel out with +2 percent noise returns and your daily average return of 0.04 percent cumulated over the year explains much more of your annual total returns.

As a consequence, an unskilled manager is as likely as a skilled manager to outperform the market if the investment horizon is as short as one day because short-term variations are driven more by noise than by fundamentals. However, a skilled manager is more likely to outperform an unskilled manager if the investment horizon is as long as ten years. Thus, the impact of luck fades over time. Unfortunately, it never totally disappears. This is an unavoidable reality of our investing world.

Investors and managers often significantly underestimate the impact of luck on investment performance. It may cause investors to make allocation decisions that are ill advised and needlessly increase the turnover of managers and strategies in their portfolios. For example, evidence shows that after a few years of underperformance, investors often feel pressured to change their allocation and substitute their managers, quite often with dreadful timing. It may also lead to overconfidence and even arrogance about one's abilities as an asset manager. The objective of this book is to demonstrate how important it is to untangle the relevant dimensions that explain success or failure in investing.

The bottom left box in figure 1.1 shows that investment outperformance can be attributed to luck, skills, or more realistically to both. Daniel Kahneman, the psychologist winner of the 2002 Nobel Memorial Prize in Economic Sciences, said that success is attributed to talent and luck while great success is the result of a little more talent and lots of luck![3] Carefully distinguishing luck from skills requires that we properly understand what the skill component is made of.

This leads us to the rightmost boxes in figure 1.1 in which we examine the components of investment skills. In chapter 5 we explain three sources of excess performance. The performance of many financial products can be explained through these sources of performance. Each is related to a form of diversification.

First, long-term performance can be obtained by diversifying unrewarded risk. Risks such as a report indicating Volkswagen has cheated on its pollution emission standards or a report indicating an existing medication has significant positive side effects can have a strong negative or positive stock price impact. However, the possibility of such idiosyncratic risks is simply not reflected in the price of securities because these risks are random and positive and negative events can presumably be diversified. However, diversifying these unrewarded risks more efficiently improves long-term return through the effect of return compounding.

Second, long-term performance can be obtained by better diversifying sources of risk that are rationally compensated with positive returns on average. We invest in equity instead of cash because we expect to be compensated for bearing market risk in the long term. There are many sources of compensated risks. Given your investment objectives and preferences, a more efficient exploitation of these sources of risk improves portfolio performance.

Finally, long-term performance can be obtained by better diversifying the risk of irrational mispricings in financial markets. *Mispricing* is the term used to express the difference between the market price of an asset and its true fundamental values. The dot-com bubble of the late 1990s is the best historical example of irrational mispricing, but mispricings are always present. Though irrational mispricings are hard to discern, you can improve your performance by adopting a portfolio structure that is more neutral to mispricings.

So-called smart beta products and many fundamental managers are consciously or unconsciously emphasizing one of these forms of diversification. As an illustration, table 1.1 presents the emphasis of different financial products and management styles on these three specific forms of diversification. If you are unfamiliar with these diversification concepts and with these products, don't worry. They will be explained in chapter 5 and put in practice in chapter 6.

Several observations come out of this table. First, each of these products claim to focus on one investment aspect. But they may, of course, pick up different sources of performance. For example, an equal weight allocation (second row)—an approach based on allocating the same amount to each of the security in your investment universe—is often proposed as a naïve but surprisingly effective way to diversify unrewarded risk (second column). But it also ensures by construction that mispriced securities are not attributed undue weight in a portfolio by allocating the same amount to each asset (third column).

Second, different approaches and methodologies can be used to exploit a specific source of performance. For instance, both maximum diversification and minimum volatility focus on diversifying unrewarded risk. Finally, if we understand the potential of all three sources of performance, there are no reasons to focus on only one of them. The issue becomes about determining how to combine them into one appropriate portfolio, which is the subject of chapter 6.

TABLE 1.1 Main sources of performance of various investment products

Product	Diversification of unrewarded risk	Diversification of priced sources of risk	Diversification of mispricing risk
Fundamental indexing			X
Equal weight allocation	X		X
Maximum diversification	X		
Low/minimum volatility	X	X	
Equal risk premia	X	X	
Value-oriented fund		X	X

Chapter 5 is not revolutionary in its ideology. It simply reminds us that once we have properly combined these sources of performance into a portfolio, there is not much more that can be done to reliably improve performance. The balance is luck. This framework can be used to explain the excess performance of most financial products and professional fund managers, and indeed finance academics and many investment experts use it. We are merely presenting sources of performance other than luck in a coherent way. Few financial products consciously exploit all three sources of performance partly because few investors emphasize or even understand all three. However, a greater understanding of all sources of performance will help democratize the investment management process and make it harder for the industry to charge greater fees. This is true of the traditional asset management industry, but even more so of a large segment of the alternative fund industry where the strategies exploited by a majority of hedge funds do not warrant high fees. In most cases, hedge funds simply apply many of the same diversification approaches we discuss in this book, but with a more permissive investment policy than allowed to a traditional manager.

To illustrate our discussion, chapter 6 presents detailed case studies. We present both the implementation of a relatively unconstrained portfolio that can be adopted by a sophisticated institution and a constrained portfolio more suited to a retail investor who faces higher transaction costs. The first is based on a sophisticated set of methodologies and programming tools, whereas the second could be implemented by an investor having access to nothing more than ETFs and an Excel spreadsheet. Our objective is to show the performance of portfolios that combine all three sources of performance and are applied to balanced portfolios of equity, fixed income, commodities, and currencies.

Of course, these sources of diversification allow for different degrees of skills. An investor might have a superior understanding of sources of risk that are priced, that is, compensated with positive returns on average, or he may have a superior ability to spot when one of these sources of priced risk will have better risk-adjusted returns. It is entirely possible that some managers outperform through their unique investment skill (bottom right box in figure 1.1). But it is also likely that some managers will attribute their success to the wrong reasons. They may attribute their success to specific attributes and to forecasting abilities that they believe are unique to them. After all, they need to justify their fees. In many cases, however, their success is caused by one or more characteristics of their portfolio structuring process, whether they are aware of this or not. In other words, successful managers may simply have a good portfolio-structuring process and some may not fully understand the implications of their process. Their general investment process and philosophy and not their specific skills drive performance.

The examples presented in chapter 6 are based on relatively simple techniques, but they nonetheless lead to appealing performance given the embedded risk. This book aims to present a short but comprehensive presentation of asset management. More sophisticated techniques can be used, but the investment principles discussed in this book remain.

Investors' Education and Behavior

There is another aspect that interacts with our understanding of market structure, investment skills, and the role of luck. It is investors' education and behavior as depicted by the all-encompassing box in figure 1.1.

Even if investors were fully convinced of the investment philosophy presented in this book and attempted to fully implement it, there are many circumstances under which they will be tempted or pressured to override the process. Therefore chapter 7 deals with the psychological and behavioral dimension of the investment process, especially within asset management organizations. The chapter also discusses how this dimension impacts our perception of the industry, the pricing of assets, and our perception of the nuances between the traditional fundamental approach to asset management and the systematic process–oriented approach (often inaccurately referred to as simply "quantitative"). For example, Paul Meehl, one of the greatest psychologists of the twentieth century, discussed how clinicians defend their predictions as being dynamic, global, and holistic while they demonize statistical approaches as being mechanical, atomistic, incomplete, and dry. Similarly, many asset managers, consultants, and investors do not understand that the investment process, that is, how we structure and diversify portfolios, matters as much as the exact methodology used to implement it. Good processes can be found in many asset management approaches, either fundamental or quantitative, but often at very different prices.

Therefore the investment guidelines discussed in this book must be sold not only to investors, but also to asset managers. A few years ago, the CIO of an investment firm asked us if this book could also address what is required to build an investment group that believes in process-based management and how to sell the approach to investors and investment committees. This is a challenging question. We know it starts and ends with education about the evidential consensus about managers' probabilities of success (fewer than 30 percent outperform in the long term), the fallacy of relying on pointwise forecasts of events (such as explicit return forecasts) to build portfolios, understanding how diversification works (diversification reduces risk and increases compounded returns), and understanding our own human weaknesses and biases (which make the implementation of a rational investment process difficult). We hope this book is a significant step toward this educational objective.

Most of the relevant work on these topics exists in either the academic or practitioner literature. The issue is integrating and properly communicating this knowledge. Otherwise, our own behavior biases will pollute the investment decision process and could become, over the long run, a much more important determinant of investors' performance at the expense of investment skills.

Investors' emotions and behavioral biases may cause prices to differ from their fundamental values. For example, the so-called technology bubble of the late 1990s is often credited to the irrational exuberance of market participants (investors, managers, and analysts). Yet in figure 1.1, the effects of "investor education and behavior" are attributed to all dimensions of our framework and not only to the mispricing of assets. It is important to realize that the behavior of investors may impact asset prices not only through their trading and investment behavior, but also through the ways asset management firms evolve and the asset management industry is structured.

Hence we end this book by suggesting ways to circumvent these difficulties. Although it is difficult to abstract ourselves fully from emotions such as fear and greed, better education should lead to more rational behavior. Better education should keep us from repeating the same mistakes too often. Understanding all the components of figure 1.1 is the true road to success.

Relevant experience and evidence is crucial to our effort in building a reliable body of knowledge. This book is a transparent and honest effort that discusses industry, asset pricing, and behavioral issues. It seeks to improve on portfolio management processes and industry practices. Hence this book is not concerned with the search for skills but instead in having the relevant structural qualities within investment portfolios that lead to long-term performance. Our skill is simply a thorough understanding and use of existing sources of long-term performance. By the end of this book, you should be convinced that it is a lot easier to believe in efficient portfolio structures as a source of performance than in our ability to consistently outperform by a unique ability to forecast which security, sector, country, or asset class will do best in the next three months.

2

Understanding the Playing Field

BEFORE WE LOOK AT the characteristics of market-beating managers and the structure of well-performing portfolios, let's understand the playing field investors face in financial markets. The stock market is often compared to a casino. We could not disagree more with this analogy. A casino is one of the few places where players know the probabilities and the odds they are facing (at least in a legal casino). Financial markets are actually quite different.

For example, in a game played with a six-sided die, the odds of rolling a specific number are 5:1 (i.e., a probability of one over six). If you throw the die twice and each throw is independent of the others, the probability of getting the same number is 1/36 (1/6 times 1/6). In a game in which you can win \$100 if you roll your chosen number twice in a row or lose \$1 otherwise, you know that your expected gain is $(1/36) \times \$100 + (35/36) \times -\$1 = \$1.81$. A "financially rational" player would be willing to pay less than \$1.81 to play this game because he would like to be compensated for taking the risk of losing \$1. Players more averse to risk would be willing to pay less than more aggressive players, say \$1 instead of \$1.50.

Investing in an asset is similar: you pay an initial amount, the market price, and you receive an uncertain payoff. Yet it is also different: both the payoff and the associated odds are unknown. When investing in equity, not only do we not know with certainty the dividends that will be received and the eventual sale price, but we also do not know the probabilities associated with these potential payoffs. Entry-level textbook probability theory does not apply directly to financial markets; there are many more layers of complexity involved in investing in financial markets.

Guaranteed Lifetime Withdrawal Benefit (GLWB) contracts are a good example of the complexity of the potential payoffs associated with some financial products. GLWBs are variable annuity contracts offered by insurance companies, designed to provide future retirees with a guaranteed minimum annual income. For example, a GLWB contract could allow a fifty-five-year-old individual to invest $1,000,000 (defined as the initial benefit base) in an investment portfolio and be guaranteed a bonus of 5 percent of the initial benefit base per year for ten years until retirement (such as at sixty-five years old) even if the portfolio underperforms the guaranteed bonus. Hence the minimum benefit base at retirement would be $1,500,000 (+ 50 percent). During retirement, the investor would receive a minimum annual income of 5 percent of his benefit base for life, resulting in a guaranteed minimum yearly cash flow of $75,000 ($1,500,000 × 5 percent). The benefit base is not a value the investor can necessarily withdraw for cash. It is simply the metric used to calculate yearly income in these contracts.

Age 55	Investment = Initial Benefit Base	$1M
Age 65	Minimum Benefit Base at Retirement	$1.5M = $1.0M + 10 × $50,000
Age 66 +	Guaranteed Minimum Yearly Income	$75,000 = $1.5M × 5 percent

The appeal of GLWBs is that the benefit base has the potential to increase faster than the minimum guarantee if the investment portfolio performs well. Therefore investors get security through the guaranteed minimum income and participation in the market through the potential increase in the benefit base. For example, the benefit base can be periodically reset (such as every year or every three years) at a higher level if the value of the portfolio net of withdrawals is above the current benefit base. Finally, because investors are offered a guaranteed income, conservative investors are often told they could tolerate riskier portfolios to target higher expected returns. For example, they could move from a 40/60 allocation to equity and fixed income to a 70/30, the most aggressive allocation often allowed in these products.[1]

It all seems very attractive. However, let's consider a few facts. On the one hand, an investment of $1,000,000 at age fifty-five leading to a minimum yearly income of $75,000 for life starting at age sixty-six represents an annualized internal rate of return of only 2.03 percent if you live until age eighty-five and capital has been depleted. The internal rate of return would increase to 2.86 percent if you live until ninety. If you live until ninety-five, it would be 3.40 percent. On the other hand, the total annual fees on GLWB contracts can be significantly higher than 3 percent when you add the fees related to investment products, guarantees, distribution, and marketing. The combination of high fees, cash withdrawals after retirement, a reset mechanism, and market uncertainty makes it difficult to forecast how the annual income could evolve beyond the minimum guaranteed level of $75,000. The income investors can expect is very much path dependent. In other words, it depends both on the cumulative performance of the portfolio and on how this performance is achieved over time because the reset of the benefit base occurs on specific dates at specific intervals. Investors in such products are usually provided with scenarios of expected yearly income under different financial conditions, but it is hard for most potential buyers to properly grasp the distribution of expected payoffs and the long-term impact of high fees on the evolution of the benefit base. Not surprisingly, the product documentation almost never explains how the participant would have done had he invested in less expensive investment alternatives over his lifetime.

Andrew Ang[2] of Columbia Business School, now at Blackrock, refers to these products as complicated, expensive, and difficult for consumers to navigate. Others use more colorful language to describe them. Hence if you thought this example was complicated, it is because the product itself is truly complex, and yet it is sold to the average investor. Of course, investors in these products do not have the option of improving their investment skills over time. Buying such products is often done once and its consequences are experienced over a lifetime.

Many risk-averse investors understandably prefer to pay high fees to ensure a guaranteed level of income during retirement. Although the investment needs are fulfilled by these products, the decision to invest in them is difficult to make. You have to form an idea about the different possible market performances over a long term and the likelihood of each scenario, as well as understand how the payoff structure will interact in each case. Finally, you must judge whether these products remain a good deal against other alternatives given the fees charged. It's complicated.

In the spring of 2010, a friend looking to invest in a similar product asked for advice. It was necessary to read the eighty-page documentation twice to fully understand the specific terms of the product and its fee structure. The most relevant problem was not to determine how the product would behave under different scenarios of market returns. Instead it was to determine if a cheaper and more conservative product not providing any guarantee was likely to outperform the proposed GLWB under most scenarios.

First, the analysis showed that the minimum payoff of this GLWB (up to the age of ninety-five) could be matched by investing 70 percent of the portfolio in a few government coupon bonds of different maturities and in one long-term fixed income ETF.

The balance of the portfolio (30 percent) would be invested in equity ETFs. Second, the analysis concluded that the income generated by this low-cost portfolio would likely outperform the GLWB unless the average yearly equity performance was either above 12 percent or less than 2 percent for several decades. Thus it was unnecessary to make predictions about market returns or managers' skills to reach the conclusion that the payoff structure of this particular product was not attractive. High fees cannot be the solution to the well-being of investors. They also make it harder to live up to financial promises because higher fees increase the likelihood that the minimum guarantee may be needed. Higher fees also reduce the income that could be expected beyond that guarantee. These comments also apply to many hedge funds and especially funds of funds that charge an extra layer of fees.

The structure of possible payoff in a game of dice is easy to compute. That of GLWBs is complex. The complex structure obscures that a similar expected payoff pattern can sometimes be achieved using a simpler portfolio approach managed in an Excel spreadsheet. It is our experience that many investors in GLWBs—and perhaps sellers of these products—did not consider or did not understand this possibility. This is a case of information asymmetry in which investors have far less relevant information than required to make an informed decision.

Complex investment processes can be intimidating, and many investors prefer to pay handsomely for advice, regardless of its usefulness. We are not saying that investing is simple or that advisory services are not worth their price. However, as will be discussed in chapter 3, only a small proportion of fund managers can outperform after fees by design and not by chance. Furthermore, investors should not have to pay high fees for investment solutions that are like target-date funds or standard balanced portfolios. There are index funds and ETFs or combinations of both that deliver effective and complete portfolio solutions for less than 0.5 percent in total expenses. They can be as balanced as dedicated portfolio solutions offered by large financial institutions and advisors.

Lussier remembers advising an entrepreneur who had $50 million in liquid assets and was earning $7 million in yearly cash flows from his business that

- He was paying at least twice as much as was reasonable in fees to his advisor. His portfolio had no distinctive advantage over what could be assembled from a few ETFs and specific securities. It already contained several ETFs, and it was under-diversified on the equity side.
- He would likely perform just as well (before fees) if he invested in a balanced portfolio of ETFs and spent two mornings each year rebalancing his portfolio.

Though the entrepreneur knew that he was overpaying for these services, it was difficult to convince him that a simple self-administered process would do as well as the unexceptional portfolio his manager had designed for him. This is far from a unique situation. Investing is intimidating even to entrepreneurs.

These examples illustrate the importance of understanding the basic structure of the market before making any decisions about the potential impact of expertise. They also illustrate that not all investments offer fair odds. If details of a specific situation seem too complicated and structurally unfavorable, it may be wise to simply stay out of it.

To Be or Not to Be Active?

Let's make a deal. We will use one equation to simplify our discussion over the next few chapters. In exchange, we promise not to use any other equations until chapter 5. To some of you, this equation will introduce many of the concepts floating around the investment world: alpha versus beta, large bets versus diversification, risk premium versus idiosyncratic risk, etc. To other readers who are already investment experts, the equation will summarize all these concepts and structure our discussion on market structure in this chapter, on delegated management in the next chapter, on forecasting in chapter 4, and on sources of performance in chapter 5.

Let's say you invest in an asset, say a stock, bond, mutual fund, hedge fund, commodity futures contract, etc. Whether you look at the value of your investment after one minute or after one year, your realized return R is the gain that you have realized through price appreciation and cash flows that you have received. For example, if you buy a stock for $100, sell it for $105 after one year, and receive a $5 dividend, then R = 10 percent. To better understand the sources of returns of any asset, we use the following representation for returns, which we will call our return equation:

$$R = R_f + \beta_m \times F_m + \beta_2 \times F_2 + \ldots + \alpha + \varepsilon.$$
$$= \text{Risk-Free Rate} + \text{Compensation for Risks}$$
$$+ \text{Mispricing} + \text{Noise/Luck}$$

In this equation, the return R has several components. First is the risk-free rate of return R_f that is obtained by investing in a safe asset, for example, a short-term bond from a developed country's government. We can always park our money in this safe asset and achieve a return equal to R_f. We are interested in the return in excess of R_f that riskier assets provide because the safe asset is the natural benchmark. Clearly, an asset that has an expected return of 5 percent is not as attractive when the risk-free rate is 8 percent than when it is 2 percent.

Second, the *F*s are returns on factors that capture common—or *systematic*—sources of risk in the economy for which investors receive compensation, while the betas (βs) govern how this asset is exposed to them. The first of these factors, F_m, is the return in excess of the risk-free rate on the value-weighted market portfolio that contains all assets weighted by their market capitalization (or market value, hence the term *value-weighted*). It is called the market factor. For example, the S&P 500 is a representation of a value-weighted portfolio of large capitalization U.S. stocks. The market portfolio is simply a much broader representation of the securities market that incorporates all securities. The market obviously has a market beta of 1 with itself.

A higher β_m indicates that a security moves more in tandem with the market than another security with a lower β_m. For example, Walmart Stores (a safer stock) has a β_m of about 0.5, while Amazon (a riskier stock) has a β_m of about 1.5. Assuming, for example, that investors require a risk premium of 4 percent to be exposed to the market portfolio, the portion of return attributed to the market factor would be 0.5×4 percent $= 2$ percent for Walmart and 1.5×4 percent $= 6$ percent for Amazon.

However, a security with a lower β_m does not necessarily indicate a lower risk overall. A security with a low β_m could be sensitive to risks other than the overall market. Hence our representation for returns allows for the possibility that there may exist other common risk factors: F_2, F_3, etc. As will be discussed in chapter 5, it is now recognized that the compensation investors get for investing in an asset is linked to exposure to other risk factors than simply the market. Among the best-known empirical factors are size (a measure of the relative performance of small versus large stocks), value (the performance of stocks with a low price-to-accounting value ratio relative to stocks with a high ratio), and momentum (the relative performance of stocks that have performed well recently to stocks that have not).

Third, $\alpha + \varepsilon$ is the idiosyncratic or *unsystematic* part of the return on the asset, the portion of realized return that cannot be explained by the risk-free rate and exposure to risk factors. On the one hand, the alpha (α) is a constant, for example, a 2 percent excess return per year. A positive α implies a higher return *every period*, regardless of other factors, like a company or a hedge fund manager outperforming the market on average because his unique skills allow him to better identify mispriced securities. On the other hand, ε is a random shock that affects only this asset and no others. This shock can be favorable or unfavorable. As an example, think of a company announcing either disappointing or surprising earnings, not of broad movements in the market. Another example is the price impact of an independent study indicating the main drug sold by a pharmaceutical firm to manage sleep apnea either increases the probability of cancer or reduces it. The impact of ε on return (scale and sign) is simply unexpected. ε could also be called good or bad luck.

To obtain this equation, we are not making any unrealistic assumptions and we are not relying on an abstract economic model either. Instead it is a simple statistical way to describe returns. All the equation does is state that realized returns among different assets will differ because they have different exposures to risk factors, because they are not similarly mispriced (α), and because luck (ε) is a random and asset-specific phenomenon. Unfortunately, mispricings and noise hinder our ability to estimate the expected return required by investors in Amazon or Walmart.

We will use this return equation in various ways in this book. We now turn to the first use, which concerns one of the most enduring debates in finance: Should we be passive or active investors?

What Does It Mean to Be an Active Investor?

Should we try to pick stocks that will outperform the market? Or should we simply buy a low-cost index fund that invests in all stocks according to their relative importance in the market? Evidence shows that active investors do not outperform the market, and investors may be better off investing in passive portfolios. Yet passive investing remains an unappealing approach for many of us. Buying the market portfolio implies that we buy poor quality companies as well as good ones. Surely we can do better? Therefore let's begin by examining the issues around being active and successful.

If we sum the returns R for all assets by weighting each of them by their market capitalization (e.g., the total value of all outstanding shares of a company), we get the return on the market portfolio R_m. At this time, Apple Inc. has a market capitalization of about 600 billion U.S. dollars and therefore contributes more to the return on the market portfolio than a company with a smaller market capitalization. By taking this weighted sum over all assets, we get our return equation for the entire market portfolio. But the market return in excess of the risk-free rate F_m is already on the right-hand side of the return equation. Therefore our return equation implies that for the entire market portfolio we necessarily have: $\alpha = 0$, $\beta_m = 1$, and $\beta_2 = 0$, $\beta_3 = 0$, etc. More specifically,

$$R_m = R_f + F_m$$

This result may seem obvious, but it leads to a very important conclusion. It means that the value-weighted market portfolio of all assets has no alpha and no net exposure to risk factors other than itself, the market portfolio. We collectively own the market, and we obviously cannot collectively outperform ourselves.

A passive investor is allocated exactly as the market portfolio is, hence the term *indexing*. What does it mean to be an active investor? Being active means that we adopt a portfolio allocation that differs from the market capitalization-weighted portfolio. We can either take an active position on a stock because we believe it is mispriced (its alpha is different from zero), take an active position on a risk factor because we believe it will perform well, or both. In all cases, other investors need to take the opposite bets to ensure our collective position is that of the market portfolio. It cannot be otherwise because investors collectively are the market.

Therefore if we ignore all fees (management, transaction, custody, etc.), the aggregate performance of all active investors will be equal to that of the market and to that of each passive investor. It also means that the aggregate portfolio of all active investors has the same sensitivity to risk factors as the market (β_m of 1 and no exposure to other factors) and no alpha ($\alpha = 0$). In other words, if an investor has a greater value bias than the market (a positive beta on the value factor), another investor must have a growth bias (a negative beta on the value factor). These statements are independent of the investment horizon. Before fees, active management is what economists call a zero-sum game.

For example, let's assume that the size of the U.S. large capitalization stock universe is $10 trillion and that 20 percent of the market ($2 trillion) is owned by indexed investors. If the entire market is up by 5 percent, the 20 percent invested by index managers must also be up by 5 percent. It then follows that the 80 percent ($8 trillion) invested by all active investors must, in aggregate, be up by 5 percent for the total market to be up by 5 percent. Whether the market is up by 5 percent in one week or in one year does not change this reality. Again, this arithmetic is independent of the horizon.

When an active investor decides to take a specific bet on a stock, he can overweight it in its portfolio compared to its weight in the market portfolio. If he beats the markets, then necessarily another investor who had underweighted the stock underperforms the market. Therefore if some active investors beat the market by $1, then some active investors underperform the market by the same amount because all investors as a group must perform as the market does. This is called the arithmetic of active management or equilibrium accounting; it is a direct consequence of simple arithmetic. It is structural, not a forecast.

Why should we care about the economics of active management? Because we need to be fully aware of the strong headwind we are facing if we decide to be active investors. To outperform the market portfolio, we need to find investments with non-zero alpha, determine if we should be over- or underexposed to risk factors other than the market portfolio, or both. But we need to do it at the expense of someone else. We all have good stories about how we managed to spot a good stock before it shot up, but whether we can do it on a consistent basis is what is important. Competition among investment professionals means that this is difficult. The fact that positive investment stories are disclosed more frequently than negative ones does not change this reality.

The economics of active management are also important in properly assessing a new investment strategy. Any strategy or portfolio solution that adopts weights that are not the market capitalization weights has to be understood through this perspective. To be profitable, somebody else has to take the other side of these deviations from the market portfolio and lose on average, either by being fully aware of it or not. We will come back to this point in chapter 5.

The Impact of Costs

Active investing is even more difficult than the previous section implies. Finding positive alpha and predicting risk factors is not a costless endeavor. There is a cost in acquiring information about different companies, predicting the economic landscape, etc. Alternatively, you can delegate the management of your portfolio, that is, hire a professional fund manager who will hunt for alpha for you. But this manager will face the same challenges as you. A professionally managed fund is itself an asset with a positive or negative alpha and exposure to different risk factors. A fund's performance can also be analyzed through the lens provided by our return equation above.

Therefore when you consider the costs and fees involved in active management, our equilibrium accounting relation from the previous section becomes a *negative*-sum game. When you take a specific bet on one or many stocks, outperforming the market means that another investor underperforms. But it also means that both of your over/underperformances are reduced by the cost incurred. To be a successful investor, it is not enough to have expertise, a good understanding of investment and of financial markets, and good information. Your expertise, understanding, and information needs to be good enough to consistently beat other investors and cover the cost of acquiring this expertise and information. Similarly, if you hire an active manager to do it on your behalf, he needs to be good enough to consistently beat the market and cover its fees. Bottom line: If you want to be active and successful in the long run, you better be really good at it. Winning at the investment game in the long run is not about how much expertise you have, but how much more expertise and staying power you have than everyone else.

Let us reiterate one important point: This book is not about passive over active management. The goal is to understand the difficulties faced when you decide to be an active investor or hire an active fund manager. The poor performance of the average active individual investor and of the average active fund manager generated the popular advice that investors should invest in low-cost index funds instead. Yet not all of us can follow this advice. We need some investors to be active, do research, work hard to find information, and form opinions about different companies such that asset prices can form in the market. That low-cost index funds are a good deal for many of us investors is a consequence of market prices incorporating a lot of information about an investment. Surprisingly, this important point is often overlooked in the popular press, but it has been well known in the academic literature for more than three decades.[3] If we all behaved as though the market portfolio was unbeatable and none of us spent any resources (time and money) on trying to beat the market, the market prices would not reflect any information and it would be easy to beat the market. Hence the market has to be inefficient enough to be attractive for talented investors to gather information and make good allocation decisions. In return, this search for outperformance makes the market relatively efficient and the passive index portfolio a good investment for those of us with no special information or investment expertise. It is a delicate balance.

The issue at stake is whether you have or can identify true investment expertise, and most importantly, how much you are paying for it. There is no doubt that a brand new entry-level Mercedes is a better car than a twenty-year-old Chevrolet. But it is not necessarily a good deal if you need to pay a million dollars for the Mercedes while the Chevrolet sells for a few hundred dollars. The debate on passive versus active management is about what the investor gets in the end, not about whether individual investors or fund managers have expertise or not. There is no doubt that some managers are truly skilled at picking good investments. The relevant question is whether a positive alpha mutual fund turns into a negative alpha fund after all fees and expenses are accounted for. Another question is how the value added is split between the skilled manager and his clients once competition among funds and market frictions are added to the mix. But let's not get ahead of ourselves.

How Do Different Groups of Investors Fare?

The market is owned by different groups of investors (individuals, mutual funds, insurance companies, pension funds, hedge funds, endowment funds, and others). The distribution of equity ownership has significantly changed over the last sixty years or so. For example, individual investors used to own 92 percent of all equity in 1950. The current percentage is closer to 30 percent currently. In 1980, the share of equity owned by mutual funds was less than 3 percent, while it is closer to 23 percent today.[4]

It is possible that one group of investors is sufficiently talented to constantly beat and extract value from another group of investors. Think of mutual fund or hedge fund managers versus retail investors. Yet very little evidence exists to support such a case, especially when fees are considered. We will examine the decision to delegate and hire a professional fund manager in more detail in chapter 3, but here we look at their collective performance as a group to understand the arithmetic of active management.

Professors Eugene Fama of the Chicago Booth School of Business and Kenneth French of Dartmouth College recently conducted a study of the performance of all equity mutual fund active managers in the United States over more than two decades.[5] Whether you look at the performance of all of their mutual funds as one big portfolio or the average performance of these managers, the same conclusion is reached. They collectively perform the same as the market index before fees and underperform the market index after fees. What this means is that they as a group do not consistently extract value from another group of investors. Obviously, we never invest in the average mutual fund manager and some managers in the lot certainly add value. Chapter 3 further explores this aspect.

Other studies provide similar evidence for different groups of professional managers. Taken as a group, there is no evidence of aggregate outperformance by institutional funds sold to public and private retirement plans, endowments, foundations, and multi-employer unions[6] or by retail and institutional mutual funds that invest in international equities.[7] On this issue, the consensus is strong.

The Subtleties in the Economics of Active Management

When thinking about the odds of being successful at the active management game, it is important to keep in mind the following issues.

The arithmetic of active management does *not* say that active investors don't create value. Active investors, by gathering information about different assets to make investment decisions, choose how capital is allocated in an economy. Efficient capital allocation is crucial to economic development because it determines which projects are funded and at what cost, which contributes to improving our standards of living. The arithmetic of active management only says that active managers as a group cannot outperform the market and that for winners there are also losers as a result.

The arithmetic of active management does *not* say that half of active managers will outperform and half will underperform the market (even before fees). Actively managed funds vary widely in size and operate under various business models. Although there are approximately 8,750 open-end mutual funds in the United States and slightly more than 775 fund complexes (e.g., Fidelity and Franklin Templeton), twenty-five of these complexes control three-quarters of the assets, and the top 50 percent of funds, measured by size, control nearly 99 percent of all assets.[8] Thus it would be a mistake to assume that necessarily half the funds should outperform or underperform because they have such different sizes and investment styles.

However, the evidence does show that once fees are taken into account, fewer than 30 percent of managers do outperform their benchmark over a horizon of ten years. For example, for the ten-year period ending in December 2014, 76.5 percent of U.S. domestic equity funds were outperformed by their benchmark. The percentage for international equity funds was 79.2 percent. Fixed income funds did not do any better.[9]

When evaluating whether an active investor or a fund manager is successful, we assume that they play a fair game. In a fair game, engagement rules are coherent and respected by all. In hockey, for example, each team has six players on the ice, assuming no penalty. No team would allow their opponent to have a seventh player while they have only six. Similarly, if the objective were to understand the structure of excess returns of active managers in the large capitalization universe, a fair game would require managers to select all of the securities in their portfolio from the same population of stocks and to use a benchmark whose structure is representative of their style (such as a value benchmark for a value manager). If managers define their investment universe differently, this would not be a fair game and it would be more difficult to draw inferences about managers' expertise from their performance (such as a manager using the Russell 3000 as his universe of securities but the S&P 500 as his benchmark).

Are managers using appropriate benchmarks to measure their performance? Morningstar says its classification is based on the underlying securities in the portfolios and on specific statistics, but some funds may not fit perfectly in any specific category. Furthermore, the great multiplication of funds in the United States from about 450 in the mid-1970s to more than 8,750 today has certainly made classification more difficult. There have been several studies whose objective is to determine if mutual funds have attributes (characteristics, investment styles, risk and return measures) that are consistent with their stated mandate.

Studies found that between one-third and one-half of funds do not have attributes that are consistent with their stated mandates.[10] This observation was confirmed by our own experience.[11] In the mid-2000s, we were involved in a process to select a fairly large number of external fund managers in the equity space to create multimanager portfolios covering four geographic zones. The initial database incorporated more than 1,500 managers. Using an internal process, this number was narrowed to less than 120 managers who were subjected to a greater due diligence over a period of nearly eight months. In the end, about twenty managers were selected.

Our process for the initial screening was unusual. We did not allow the individuals involved in this project to use the managers' performances as a criterion. Recent historical performances can consciously or unconsciously impact the opinions of decision makers. However, our teams were allowed to use the performance data to determine if the actual styles of managers were consistent with their stated mandates. If it was not, they were eliminated. We found that more than one-third of all managers in our database had performance attributes that were inconsistent with their stated mandate, such as a manager in the large market capitalization segment with a significant sensitivity to small market capitalization firms.

Let's consider another real example of two large North American pension funds. In recent years, these two organizations have internally structured global equity portfolios that emphasize value and quality tilts. One institution chose to evaluate the performance of their managers against a benchmark that is adjusted for several documented risk factors *F*s. The other institution made the assumption that their process leads to a more risk-efficient portfolio than the global market, that this increased efficiency is not explained by other risk premiums, and has built a benchmark around a standard global equity index and cash. The first institution adjusted to the portfolio orientation by creating a more complete benchmark that incorporates several risk premiums, while the second simplistically assumed that there is a single risk premium and created a benchmark that managers are very likely to outperform in the long run. Thus inappropriate benchmarks may create the wrong impression that the zero-sum game argument is not valid. It can also lead to bigger managers' bonuses than what is deserved. Finally, it may artificially inflate the percentage of managers that are reported to have outperformed their benchmarks.

These observations do not change our prior statement. If most investors pursue the objective of outperforming the market, active investing still remains a negative-sum game after fees. However, some empirical observations could theoretically appear to contradict this statement if managers were using inappropriate benchmarks.

Concluding Remarks

To outperform the market portfolio, you need to be an active investor, which implies that you need to look for non-zero alpha assets and expose yourself to risk factors other than the market portfolio. To be consistently successful, you need to be better than many other investors that are playing the same game and also be good enough to cover your costs. You may also need to avoid bad luck, especially when the investment horizon is short. Intense competition among investors says that achieving such a feat is undoubtedly hard.

Why don't we simply delegate this task to specialized investment professionals? The economics of active management does not preclude one group of investors from consistently beating another group, although this possibility is not clearly supported by the evidence. While the same evidence also indicates that investment professionals as a group do not consistently outperform and that less than 30 percent of active managers outperform in the long run, surely it is possible to identify some of the most successful managers among them. The next chapter deals with this question.

3

Skill, Scale, and Luck in Active Fund Management

Mutual fund managers are talented, but on average none of that skill enriches asset owners.

—Andrew Ang, *Asset Management: A Saystematic Approach to Factor Investing*

THERE ARE SOME TALENTED and skilled fund managers out there. As discussed in the previous chapter, the market has to be inefficient enough (i.e., possible to beat) that skilled investors have the incentive to spend resources looking for mispriced securities. If you do not possess special expertise or information, or if you simply have a full-time job that is not about money management, you may decide to delegate the management of your portfolio. The issue is to identify truly skilled managers by accounting for the potential impact of luck and, most importantly, to be able to do it in advance.

There may be no better example to illustrate luck than a 2006 contest between ten Playboy Playmates that were each asked to select five stocks.[1] The winner beat the S&P 500 Index by nearly 30 percent and did better than 90 percent of money managers. Although only four Playmates outperformed the S&P 500, it was still better than the third of active managers that did. When the investing horizon is short, luck dominates performance results.

Hence looking at short time series of performance data to identify good managers and strategies is unreliable. We need an understanding of the qualities that make an investment process sustainable. This brings us to a very important question: How can we properly select a manager if we do not have a proper understanding of the sources of sustainable performance? In the spring of 2012, two commodity managers debated their respective investment styles (fundamental and quantitative) at a hedge fund conference in Montreal. The moderator was a manager for a fund of funds group. The two commodity managers had performed exceptionally well over many years. After listening to both managers, we still could not decipher why one manager should be selected over the other. In fact, despite their financial successes (unsuccessful managers are rarely invited to speak at conferences), the justifications they provided for their superior expertise were not different from what we usually hear from most managers: superior research, greater capacity to adapt to a changing environment, long experience of team members, discipline, superior risk management, better technology, etc. (you've heard all of this before). We have yet to meet a manager that does not claim to have those qualities, even the ones with less favorable track records.

The best question at this conference came from a business colleague who asked the moderator how he would choose between these two styles/managers. The answer was a few minutes long, but it can be summarized as follows: "I do not really know, but I will make sure that the manager I choose has the risk management systems in place to protect my downside." This answer seems to indicate that in the absence of a strong philosophy and a deep understanding of cause and effect, investors (even those specializing in manager selection) are stuck having to rely almost solely on past performances and on the risk-management processes of these managers to make investment decisions. Furthermore, we should not underestimate the natural attraction of investors toward managers that have interesting "stories" to tell.

Protecting the downside is important. Unfortunately, risk management has often become the main criterion by which a manager is judged. In our opinion, it is even more important to understand why a manager should be expected to perform appropriately. Professional risk management and a proper investment policy are the minimum standards that should be expected. The required standard of risk management should not be a reason to invest, but a justification not to invest.

We must address two issues. First, we will sort out the possibility that managers with no skill may outperform and that managers with skills may not, and try to establish the proportion of fund managers that are truly skilled. Second, we will discuss the evidence on performance persistence in the hopes of being able to identify those skilled managers.

The Impact of a Few Decisions

John Paulson, the hedge fund billionaire, delivered a 158 percent performance to investors through his Paulson Advantage Plus fund in 2007. He was again successful in 2008. His success in both years can be attributed to a few good dependent views: a substantial decline in the value of subprime debt and its subsequent contagion to financial institutions. However, if you were not invested with John Paulson in 2007 but, impressed by his 2007 performance, invested in the Paulson Advantage Plus fund in January 2008, your portfolio's value would have declined cumulatively by more than 36 percent over the following seven years. What should we conclude about his skills and potential for long-term performance in this case?

In a context where luck relative to skill plays a minor role in explaining performance, a small sample size may be enough to evaluate whether or not someone is skilled. However, if luck or a single glimpse of genius is a significant contributor to success, we

TABLE 3.1 Sample size required to reach a conclusion versus the nature of the activity

Sample size	Importance of luck versus skills in achieving success	
	Predominantly luck	Predominantly skills
Large Sample	Essential	Redundant
Small Sample	Useless	Sufficient

need a large sample size to arrive at the same conclusion. In his book on the impact of skill and luck in different fields,[2] Michael Mauboussin explains the relations among skills, luck, and sample size as described in table 3.1.

For example, chess is entirely about skill. A grand master will not lose against a bad player. We do not need to set a tournament of a hundred games to confirm this finding. However, when flipping a coin, it may require a large sample to conclude beyond a reasonable doubt that no one is skilled at flipping a coin. For example, if we ask one thousand individuals to flip a coin ten times, we will observe a wide distribution of results. The most common result will be five tails and five heads, but a few players will flip nine and ten heads or tails. Thus, some players may look skilled at flipping coins. However, if we ask those same players to each flip a coin a total of one thousand times, the distribution of heads and tails will narrow around 50 percent for all of them. No player will really look skilled. Because of the significant amount of noise in financial markets, success in portfolio management is closer to flipping a coin than to playing chess.

John Paulson had a great idea in shorting securities linked to subprime mortgages and then financial institutions. However, like any performance that is linked to a small sample of significant decisions, why should brilliance in recognizing and exploiting the mess in subprime translate to brilliance in trading gold, equity, or timing an economic recovery? Not only is Paulson's successful performance in 2007 and 2008 linked to few major decisions, but these decisions are also linked to different skill domains than his more recent activities. A great play is not a long-term strategic process. After the big play in subprime was over, an investor would have done much better by investing in a low-cost 60/40 portfolio. In fact, even if we consider the strong 2007 performance, the fund did not outperform a 60/40 indexed portfolio from 2007 to 2014. However, few managers of balanced portfolios become billionaires.

Furthermore, many successes in our industry are explained by the relative price cycles among securities, sectors, asset classes, and regions. These cycles can last for many years before eventually reversing. For example, figure 3.1 illustrates the relative performance of the financial sector against the energy sector using three-year cumulative excess returns. A positive value indicates that the financial sector outperformed the energy sector over the previous three years. Although we never know ahead of time how long these cycles last, they are often very long.

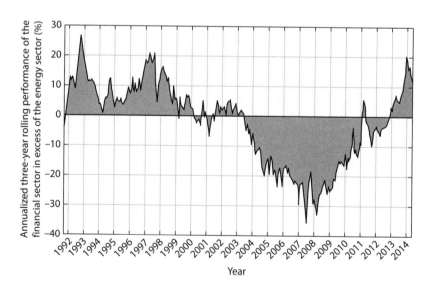

FIGURE 3.1 Annualized rolling three-year excess performance of the energy sector over the financial sector

The figure shows that the financial sector almost systematically outperformed the energy sector in the 1990s. The reverse was observed between 2002 and 2013. Thus, if a manager had taken the view in the early 1990s that financials were to outperform, he would have been right for a very long time. Once we are proven right, it reinforces our belief in our own abilities, which may incite us to further increase our allocation bets. The spreads in relative performance between securities, sectors, and asset classes can be significant. A small deviation from benchmark allocations can lead to significant excess under- or overperformance. A single decision can create winners and losers for many years. Would you assume that a manager has broad and persistent expertise and will be successful in the future because he was right on a single or a few decisions that impacted his performance for many years? As we stated before, if one thousand individuals without expertise were asked to overweight or underweight the financial sector at the expense of the energy sector, many among them will likely be right for several years even if they have no expertise. How can we separate true experts from nonexperts if both can be wrong?

According to Grinold's fundamental law of active management, confidence about a manager's ability to outperform increases when performance is attributed to a large sample of independent decisions.[3] However, as the previous examples illustrate, the fact that a manager may have made a large number of trades does not mean that these trades are truly independent. An investment process can be driven by a narrow range of common requirements leading to specific and concentrated risks even if the portfolio appears diversified. For example, a value manager may own a hundred stocks, each carefully selected, but his outperformance may be explained by how the value segment performed against the growth segment. Clearly we need a more robust way to identify truly skilled managers than just looking at recent historical returns.

What Do We Mean by Luck and Skills?

Once again, our return equation from chapter 2 can help. Think of the return R as the return of an entire fund. Exactly as we had taken a weighted sum of the return equations of all assets to obtain the return of the market portfolio in the previous chapter, we can also compute the weighted sum of the returns of all assets held by a specific manager to examine its fund's properties, more specifically its exposure to risk factors and its historical excess performance or alpha α. The fund's alpha is often used as a measure of skill. Given the exposure of the manager's portfolio to risk factors, the alpha provides a measure of the value added by the manager on a risk-adjusted basis.

However, historical alpha α is not proof of skills. Excess returns are also impacted by random shocks ε, otherwise known as good or bad luck. Luck refers to the possibility that these random shocks will falsely increase the estimated alpha in a small sample and therefore make a fund and his manager mistakenly look good. Thus, we use the terms *noise* and *luck* interchangeably. These shocks are random and unpredictable, hence the term *noise*. Luck is when these random shocks result in good performance purely by chance. Distinguishing alpha (skills) from random shocks (luck) is not a simple matter.

Luck is linked to the well-known phenomenon of regression to the mean, which has to do with the tendency of exceptional performances (good or bad) to become average over time rather than to remain exceptional. This can easily be understood by the random and unpredictable nature of shocks. If good performance is entirely caused by a random and unpredictable shock, it is less likely to be followed by another extreme favorable random shock. Thus, future performance will be less impressive and will appear to have regressed to the mean. For example, even if an individual flipped a coin ten times and got an unlikely result of ten heads, the most likely scenario if he were to flip the same coin ten more times would still be five heads and five tails.

There is already one important caveat to this aspect. We should look at *risk-adjusted returns*, not raw returns of a fund; we should control for its exposure to risk factors because a manager could easily beat the market on average by adopting, for example, a high market risk exposure β_m. Clearly we do not need to hire a manager to simply take more market risk. We can do this by ourselves. We also need to be further convinced that the excess performance of a manager is attributed to his skills and not to a consistent and specific portfolio allocation bias, which adds an undisclosed risk to the portfolio or to a benchmark that does not recognize some of the risk factors that are present in the portfolio. The example cited in chapter 2 of a large pension fund using a benchmark built from a standard global equity index and cash is a good example of this issue.

But one manager's expertise may rely on knowing when to increase or when to decrease his exposure to the market portfolio. Fortunately, this is not a problem. When we estimate the alpha of a manager, we must simply control for his average exposure to market risk. Therefore his market timing ability, if any, will show up in the α. So far, so good.

The same reasoning applies when there are multiple risk factors out there. A manager's expertise may rely on identifying these risk factors and knowing how to efficiently balance them in a portfolio. A popular mantra in the hedge fund community is "the exotic beta you don't know about is my alpha." Again, any factor allocation and timing skill will simply show up in the estimated alpha when we use standard statistical analysis that relies on constant factor exposures. Therefore we begin our investigation by looking at funds and controlling for their average exposures to risk factors. Then we will discuss factor timing abilities.

To illustrate these facts, figure 3.2 reports the cumulative value of $100 invested in the Russell 1000 Growth and $100 invested in

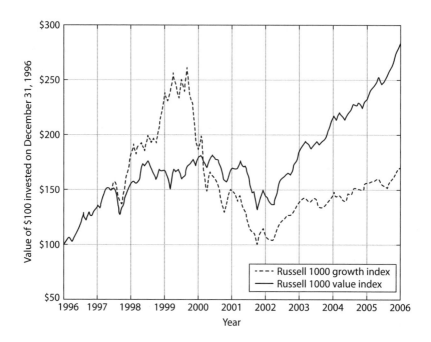

FIGURE 3.2 Russell 1000 growth versus Russell 1000 value. *Source*: Bloomberg

the Russell 1000 Value Indices over the ten years ending in 2006. The index with a growth tilt outperformed in the 1990s, whereas the index with a value tilt outperformed over the whole decade.

Now consider a manager with a strong value tilt in his portfolio. Over the whole period, he would have outperformed a manager with a strong growth tilt. But at the end of the 1990s, he would have looked comparatively bad and likely lost a lot of clients to growth managers. Significant evidence exists that value stocks do outperform growth stocks in the long run and we often use value as a risk factor F (more on this in chapter 5). But fortunately we can still properly evaluate his skills. Controlling for the exposure to this risk factor, the estimated alpha of the manager would tell us whether he added value over the whole period despite the underperformance of value stocks early on.

What if another manager had the acumen to expose his portfolio to growth during the early period and focused on value after? His average exposure to the value factor might be close to zero over the whole period, having been negative in the early part and positive later on. But his *factor timing* ability would have paid off considerably. In this case, the factor timing ability of the second manager would result in a higher estimated alpha than for the first manager, who had adopted a constant exposure to the value factor. A similar point can be made for securities like our energy and financial stocks in the previous example.

How hard is it to identify a positive alpha manager from historical performance? Figure 3.3 presents the probability of identifying a skilled manager given the number of months of performance we

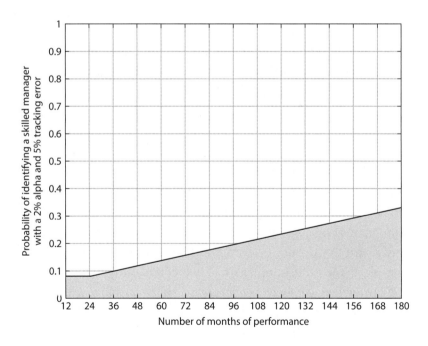

FIGURE 3.3 Probability of identifying a truly skilled manager using past performance alone

observe. In this test, we simulate the market return F_m assuming a realistic average annual excess return of 5 percent and a volatility of 20 percent, and we simulate the performance of a large number of funds, all of which have alphas of 2 percent per year and volatility of noise of 5 percent per year. The results are humbling. When we observe only one year of monthly returns and estimate a fund's alpha after the fact using standard statistical techniques, we have less than a 10 percent chance of correctly identifying a fund with a positive alpha. In other words, even though all funds in our simulation have positive alphas, we are unable to prove with reasonable statistical certainty that more than 10 percent of them have positive alphas after one year. Clearly, noise and luck play a large role in small samples. Even when we observe fifteen years' worth of performance, we can only confirm the skill of managers in about one-third of all cases. Furthermore, we can see this as the best case scenario; in this simple test, we assume that returns are statistically well behaved and that funds' alpha and market exposure are constant.[4] Reality is much less orderly. For example, funds' alphas exhibit a fat-tailed and asymmetric distribution, which further complicates the identification of skilled managers.[5]

This simple simulation shows the shortfalls of relying on a short window of performance—say three to five years—to identify skilled managers. Investing is plagued by a lot of noise, and we tend to have small samples. Yet many investors use a three-year window to evaluate whether or not to fire a manager. Investors truly underestimate the horizon (or sample size) required to derive confidence about a manager's expertise from historical returns. Firms that offer dozens or even hundreds of funds on their mutual fund platform understand this. They offer many funds because they know few of their funds are likely to remain winners for more than a few years, and having many funds ensures that there will always be some that have performed well recently. Offering too many funds may be an indication of an absence of investment philosophy.

Finally, as peculiar as this may seem, the significance of luck on outcome increases when the players are more uniformly skilled. Michael Mauboussin reports that the time spread between the first- and twentieth-rank marathon runners was about forty minutes in 1932. Today, it is no more than five to seven minutes. Eighty years ago, the best marathon runner may have dominated in almost all circumstances. Today, considering the greater pool of potential athletes and access to the best training techniques and diet, it may require more than a single race to determine who is best. Similarly, it takes more than a few years of returns to identify good managers.

How Many Skilled Managers Are There Really?

In chapter 2, we discussed a study by Eugene Fama and Kenneth French that showed that in aggregate U.S. mutual fund managers do not outperform the market at the expense of other groups of investors. Fortunately, this study also provided a statistical methodology that can distinguish skill from luck. Controlling for the amount of noise in the data, they concluded that once fees are added to the mix, very few funds have enough skills to cover their costs and provide positive net alpha to investors.

Laurent Barras of McGill University, Olivier Scaillet of the University of Geneva, and Russ Wermers of the University of Maryland provide an even more sophisticated methodology to control for luck in performance data.[6] In a sample of more than two thousand U.S. domestic equity mutual funds over the period from 1975 to 2006, they can identify only 0.6 percent of them as having a positive alpha net of fees and costs. This result appears at first damning for managers, but in fact their results show that about one out of ten managers are identified as being skilled. It is simply that despite their value added, they do not outperform a simple index once costs and fees are taken into account.

It is important to contrast these results with the evolution of the active management industry as a whole. Lubos Pastor of the Chicago Booth School of Business and Robert Stambaugh and Lucian Taylor, both at the Wharton School, examine the relations among the performance of equity fund managers, the size of their funds, and the size of their industry.[7] In the fund management industry, there may be diseconomies of scale: a larger fund may suffer from market impact when trying to execute its larger trades, and a larger size of the industry implies that more managers are chasing the same alpha opportunities.

They find evidence, though weak, that the size of a fund's assets under management seems to impede a manager's ability to outperform. This is consistent with an increasing cost structure: as a manager outperforms, he attracts new money inflows from clients, but it becomes harder for him to continue outperforming. They find strong evidence, however, that the size of the mutual fund industry negatively impacts outperformance. Managers may have become better over time, but the increase in the size of the industry implies more competition among fund managers, so it takes more skills just to keep up. The level of skill may have increased over time, there is learning on the job, and new entrants seem more skilled than incumbents, but as the industry grows, there is more competition and it becomes harder to outperform and provide investors with positive net alpha. As individual skills improve, so do the skills of the entire industry.

The results mentioned previously, that many fund managers have skills, are echoed in this study, albeit based on a different methodology. Here results show that about three-quarters of managers have skills before costs and fees and before their fund performance is impacted by their own size and by the size of the industry. But again, not much of this value added trickles down to investors' pockets.

The presence of diseconomies of scale reminds us of a meeting with a manager in New York in the summer of 2011. This manager benefitted from the subprime debacle, but his spectacular performance in 2007 and 2008 quickly turned negative and strong redemptions ensued. Much to our surprise, this manager said that "the problem with producing a greater than 100 percent return in a short period of time is first that your assets double [from performance] and second that they increase further [because everyone suddenly wants to invest with you] but it does not mean you know what to do with all this capital." Unfortunately, they did not.

A recent study by Jonathan Berk at Stanford University and Jules van Binsbergen at the Wharton School argues that neither gross nor net (after fees have been removed) alpha are appropriate measures of skill.[8] Instead, they use gross dollar value added. Net alpha can be driven to zero due to competition, and the link between skill and gross alpha is not obvious. For example, Peter Lynch, while managing the highly successful Magellan fund, generated a 2 percent gross *monthly* alpha on average assets under management of $40 million during his first five years of tenure and a 0.20 percent alpha per month during his last five years on assets of about $10 billion. Looking at gross alpha would imply he may have lost his edge, while in fact he went from creating $1 million per month to more than $20 million per month in value.

This study is noteworthy for many reasons. First, it looks at a large sample of all actively managed mutual funds based in the United States, including those that invest in international stocks. Second, it uses not only standard risk factors to control for risk, but also alternatively Vanguard Index funds that were available in the market at the time when the fund performances were realized. Standard risk factors, such as value or momentum (to be discussed in chapter 5), are subject to criticisms: they involve both a large number of long and short positions that may be difficult to trade and it is likely that most investors did not fully know about their existence a few decades ago. Hence they recognize that it may be unfair to measure funds' net alpha using risk factors that were not genuinely part of their investment opportunity set then.

Beyond confirming that the average manager is skilled, the analysis also shows that the difference across managers in their measure of skills (dollar value added) persists for up to ten years. Therefore it may be possible to identify them well in advance, which is a task we examine more closely in the next section.

Can We Identify Skilled Managers in Advance?

Now that we have established that there are skilled fund managers out there, although few outperform after fees, can we identify them in advance? We could compute their alpha using past performances and invest in high alpha funds. But this method assumes past alpha is indicative of future alpha. Therefore we first need to determine if there is persistence in managers' skills. Of course, tracking funds that show persistence in returns may appear profitable, but it may also incur a significant amount of manager turnover and transition costs.

As alluded to in the previous section, α is also not the whole story. We also care about the risk embedded in the random idiosyncratic shocks ε. We usually quantify this risk by computing the standard error (i.e., a measure of risk) of these shocks, which is usually referred to in the industry as the tracking error. Tracking error expresses the volatility of the performance unexplained by the exposure to the market factor. A fund with a 1 percent annual tracking error would have performance that would remain within ±2 percent of the index most of the time. Funds that track an appropriately defined index will have an annualized tracking error lower than 1 percent, and highly active funds' tracking error can easily reach 5 to 10 percent per year. Some managers called themselves active but have tracking errors as low as 2 percent. They are often referred to as benchmark huggers or closet indexers. They get paid significant fees for holding portfolios that are very much like the index.

Again, we would like to identify a manager that truly has a positive alpha, but given his alpha, we prefer a manager who can achieve this outperformance without taking significant risk relative to his benchmark (i.e., a lower tracking error). Furthermore, for a given level of fees, we prefer a manager that takes more tracking error than less assuming the same alpha efficiency per unit of tracking error. To summarize these two effects, we can compute the ratio of the alpha to the tracking error—the *information ratio*—of which a higher value indicates a better manager. Unfortunately, because the performance related to idiosyncratic shocks (i.e., luck) in a specific fund can be confused with alpha, a high information ratio can also be partly explained by luck. Therefore it may not be indicative of high future risk-adjusted returns.

Nevertheless, the same sophisticated econometric techniques mentioned in the previous section can help successfully identify future well-performing funds based on past performance alone.[9] But we are faced with two problems. First, there is little evidence of performance persistence based on fund returns alone. If anything, it seems to be mostly concentrated among poorly performing funds that tend to underperform again in the future. Second, in addition to the knowledge and expertise required to handle these econometric techniques, investors should carefully assess the costs of switching their investment across funds.

We can improve our chances of identifying a good manager in advance by exploiting what we know about skilled managers. For example, we know that managers that have displayed skills historically were good stock pickers during bull markets *and* exhibited good factor timing skills during recessions.[10] During booms, these skilled managers focus on analyzing companies and choosing their investments, and during recessions they adequately hold more cash and emphasize defensive sectors. Characterizing funds according to their stock-picking ability during booms and their factor-timing ability during recessions allows us to pick funds that will outperform up to one year in the future. Note that we are also still subject to small sample biases as there are very few economic cycles to evaluate their performance and many organizational changes may have occurred even if they have a twenty-year track record.

There are also other measures based on holdings rather than returns that can be used to forecast managers' outperformance. For example, the *active share* measure[11] captures the total absolute weight deviation of a fund from its benchmark weights (multiplied by one-half to avoid double counting). In essence, it is a measure of the degree of similarity between a portfolio and its benchmark. An active share of zero indicates that a portfolio is identical to its benchmark, while an active share of one indicates a portfolio whose structure is totally different from its benchmark. Imagine, for example, that the benchmark is composed of two stocks, Walmart and Amazon, with respective weights of 40 percent and 60 percent. A manager allocating an equal amount to both would have an active share of 10 percent (0.5 × (50 percent – 40 percent + 60 percent – 50 percent)), whereas one investing only in Walmart would have an active share of 60 percent (0.5 × (100 percent – 40 percent + 60 percent – 0 percent)).

Results suggest that outperformance is strong for funds with a high level of active share (such as 0.80 or above), that is, for benchmark-agnostic managers. It could be that high active share funds exhibit knowingly or unknowingly some of the forms of diversification that will be discussed in chapter 5. Because active share is persistent across time for a fund, it could be used to forecast a fund's future outperformance.

This measure has come under scrutiny lately as high active share funds tend to be funds that invest in small-capitalization stocks whose index has had a negative risk-adjusted performance over the study's period.[12] In other words, the link between active share and fund performance may simply be due to the poor performance of U.S. small-cap indexes during this period, not to the outperformance of funds benchmarked on these indexes. Computing active share with respect to the market-cap weighted portfolio of the stocks chosen by the manager avoids having to identify the benchmark and robustly predicts future outperformance.[13] Nevertheless, active share is an efficient way to distinguish between genuine stock pickers and closet indexers. For example, a portfolio with a 20 percent active share is similar to investing 80 percent of the assets in the index and 20 percent in something that is different from the index. Hence if you are paying significant fees to this manager, you are paying to have only one-fifth of your portfolio actively managed!

Finally, there is a wide variety of other characteristics linked to outperformance. They are the ones you would intuitively expect: longer education and experience (SAT scores, better MBA program, PhD, CFA title), managers' experience in large funds, funds operating within a flatter organizational structure, a higher amount of manager's money invested into their fund, a more widespread network of the fund managers, funds that invest locally or concentrate in specific industries, etc.[14]

However, identifying performing managers from statistical analyses of past performances or from other indicators such as active share or organizational structure still remains a challenge. There is simply too much noise that can impact the performance of a single manager, even over longer periods—five years, for example. This is why chapter 5 is dedicated to identifying the relevant skills and structural causes of outperformance of top managers and products.

The Reasons Investors Still Invest with Active Managers

The previous section suggests that identifying good managers in advance requires an advanced knowledge of economics, econometrics, and precise data about a fund's characteristics and holdings. If an investor has such expertise, maybe he is also in a position to apply such knowledge to building his own portfolio instead of identifying good managers!

It is not necessarily surprising that a large fraction of our wealth remains invested in actively managed funds. This fact is consistent with a context in which investors learn slowly about the level of managers' skills and in which there are diseconomies of scale. As the size of the active management industry increases, competition makes it harder for fund managers to outperform. But as its size decreases, more market inefficiencies appear, and active managers outperform passive indexes.[15] Again, there is a delicate balance.

Although the evidence against net outperformance is strong, firms are skilled at marketing their products in a much more favorable light. For example, Andrew Ang refers to a survey by PERACS (a provider of private equity fund analytics and track record certification) indicating that 77 percent of private equity firms declare to have top-quartile performance, an observation that defies the numbers. Charles Ellis, the well-known investor and founder of Greenwich Associates, rounded up the parties responsible for the current state of affairs[16] as follows.

Investment managers are skilled at presenting their performance in a favorable light. For example, they may choose the historical period for performance that makes the best impression (five years, seven years, or ten years) depending on what looks best. In the case of firms offering a multifund platform, they may concentrate their marketing on those funds that performed best in recent years. Finally, even simple investment processes are presented in a compelling fashion, giving the impression that some managers have developed a true competitive advantage when in fact there may be little that differentiates them from others.

Also, the consultant business model is based on maximizing the present value of future advisory fees, which is in many cases inconsistent with advising clients not to make significant changes to their portfolios and to remain consistent. Furthermore, consultants are known to shift their recommendations toward managers that have performed well recently. As Ellis mentioned, how often have you heard a consultant say the following:

While this manager's recent performance record certainly does not look favorable, our professional opinion is that this manager has weathered storms in a market that was not hospitable to her style and has a particularly strong team that we believe will achieve superior results in the future.

Finally, within investment committees and senior management, there is often the belief that when performances are disappointing, something must be done. The pressure on internal management to act can be significant. When consultants are hired, they will often support the need for change, as many consultants will find proper justification for what management wants. Lussier has witnessed this many times. After all, this is how advisory fees are generated. Because most investment committee members do not have the depth of understanding required to challenge those advisors and consultants (a subject that will be discussed in chapter 7), they can easily be impressed and influenced by forty-page binders of data and charts.

To support this point, consider the results from a study by Amit Goyal at HEC Lausanne and Sunil Wahal at Arizona State University, who look at the performance of fund managers before and after plan sponsors fired them (table 3.2). Most managers that had performed poorly prior to being fired performed much better after they were fired.

TABLE 3.2 Cumulative excess returns of managers before and after being fired (1996–2003) (%)

Before being fired		After being fired	
Timing	Performance	Timing	Performance
Years −3 to 0	+2.27	Years 0 to 1	+0.98
Years −2 to 0	−2.06	Years 0 to 2	+1.47
Years −1 to 0	−0.74	Years 0 to 3	+3.30

Source: Amit Goyal and Sunil Wahal, "The Selection and Termination of Investment Management Firms by Plan Sponsors," *Journal of Finance* 63 (2008): 805–47.

Concluding Remarks

We mentioned in the introduction that fewer than 30 percent of active managers outperform over horizons such as five to ten years. This level is independent of the level of expertise that exists in the market. It is structural. As long as fees stay at similar levels, our likelihood of identifying performing managers will likely remain below 30 percent. However, we also concluded in this chapter that it is a challenge to identify which managers will be part of the winning group. Historical performances are not an efficient guideline of future performance.

The industry is certainly aware of the reality that few managers outperform their own fees. Many asset managers fear that more and more investors will turn to cheaper indexed and passive investment solutions. As decades have passed, the alignment of interests between investors and service providers has declined. The SEC used to believe that public ownership of mutual fund companies was a violation of fiduciary duties. Today, following a 1958 ruling that overruled the SEC position, more than 80 percent of the largest forty mutual fund complexes are public. Consequently, more and more asset management firms have a dual role of seeking a return on corporate capital and upholding their mandate to serve the interests of investors. Consequently, the number of funds has exploded, as has the failure rate, which increased from 1 percent per year in the 1960s to 6 percent per year in the last decade. Furthermore, even though the average size of mutual funds has increased, the average expense ratio of equity funds doubled from 1960 to 2010.[17]

As we started this chapter with a quote from Andrew Ang, we will close it with another from him. In his book on asset management, he mentions that "killing or merging poorly performing funds is the only way the marketing team of the firm Janus can say with a straight face, '100 percent of Janus equity funds have beaten their benchmark since inception.'" The objective of many fund complexes is often to kill underperforming funds and to have enough funds so that some of them will always have good historical performances. This is not a basis to build a business that will confidently serve investors better.

4

What May and Can Be Forecasted?

FORECASTING IS UNAVOIDABLE IN portfolio management. Even when we do not rely on explicit forecasts such as "the stock market is expected to outperform bonds over the next year," we use implicit forecasts. If we invest in the stock market, we implicitly forecast that it is better than investing in anything else such as putting it in a risk-free asset. For example, investing in an equity fund instead of a fixed income fund may be motivated by the fact that stocks have historically outperformed safer assets, and we implicitly predict that historical average returns are adequate guidance for future relative performance and that equity prices integrate an adequate risk premium.

What actually varies in forecasting is the degree of sophistication in the forecasting methodology used. The key thing for investors is to know to what extent complexity and sophistication in forecasting methodologies should be used. We touched on the subject of forecasting in chapter 3, but forecasting can be used for more than simply selecting fund managers. Whether you allocate between mutual funds, between different assets, or between risk factors, you need to forecast their respective rewards (expected return) and risks to determine a properly balanced allocation among them.

It is important to begin by understanding what we are actually doing when we attempt to predict. If we could precisely forecast actual events, things would be extremely simple. We could simply adjust our portfolio according to what is going to happen; for example, invest all our wealth in the next Apple. But events are random, and by definition realizations of random variables cannot be forecasted, otherwise they wouldn't be called random. What *may* be forecasted are the properties of probabilities associated with these events.

This basic distinction is crucial. Claiming an event is going to happen is meaningless unless we specify that it has a 100 percent probability of happening (i.e., it is the only event possible). What we may forecast are characteristics of the distribution of probabilities of different events such as the *expected distribution* of returns for specific stocks, indices, or factors. For example, we may say that the expected return for the S&P 500 twelve-month forward is 8 percent with a 10 percent likelihood of a return below –10 percent and a 2.5 percent likelihood of a return below –20 percent, but we cannot forecast the actual realized returns. The distribution of possible returns may be expressed by its variance or quantiles (e.g., the median or the 1 percent or 5 percent quantile used in finance for risk measures such as the Value-at-Risk). Hence it is important to understand what is actually being forecasted.

This distinction brings another crucial issue: assessing a forecast's accuracy. If we forecast a high of 77 degrees for a summer day in New York, but the temperature hits 80, we cannot conclude that we are wrong. Only after a *series* of forecasts can our forecasting ability be evaluated. After fifty forecasts of daily temperature, are we on average correct? Is our average forecast error close to zero? Other criteria for evaluating forecasting accuracy include the variance of forecast errors and the degree of the worst forecast error.

Despite the impossibility of forecasting actual realized value, many experts still attempt to make explicit point forecasts, such as the S&P 500 will rise by 10 percent next year. Hence, although we should now understand what may be forecasted, this chapter presents evidence on our inability to make explicit point forecasts and also deals with what *can* be forecasted. We start with the easiest way to make predictions: asking experts for theirs. Then we move to the other side of the spectrum, which is about using only statistical predictions. We contrast the evidence on forecasts resulting from personal expertise to statistical models in different domains. We also discuss whether greater complexity and sophistication in forecast methodologies lead to more precise and useful forecasts.

We Know Less Than We Think

The easiest route is to use predictions made by experts. If economists predict favorable economic conditions over the next year, we might allocate more to riskier assets in our portfolio. As will become clear, the identification of skilled professional forecasters is plagued with several problems, many of which are the same ones that complicate the selection of skilled fund managers discussed in chapter 3.

There is not yet good evidence that we are able to accurately forecast the dynamics of complex systems. Nassim Taleb describes our record concerning these forecasts as dismal and marred with retrospective distortions;[1] we usually only understand risk after a significant negative event. In 2006, the political scientist Philip Tetlock of the University of Pennsylvania published a landmark book on the forecasting accuracy of 284 so-called experts who made their livings offering advice on political trends.[2] The study contained no fewer than 28,000 predictions, gathered over a period of more than eighteen years, in which experts were asked to attribute probabilities to three alternative outcomes. These experts were generally no more skilled than the layperson. When experts determined that an event had no chance of occurring, it would occur 15 percent of the time. If they were 80 percent certain that an event would occur, it would occur 45 percent of the time. Twenty-five percent of events that were a sure thing would not occur at all. Their average performance was worse than if equal probabilities had been attributed to all events. These observations do not mean that experts lack a mastery of their subject matter; rather, this knowledge does not translate to better prediction making.

Nate Silver analyzed 733 political forecasts made by John McLaughlin and his panelists on the TV show *The McLaughlin Group*.[3] On average, 39 percent of their predictions were completely true, 37 percent were completely false, with the balance accounted by mostly true, mostly false, and in between answers. Individual panelists did no better.

Economic forecasting is not much more accurate. In November 2014, the Montreal CFA Society invited former Federal Reserve chairman Ben Bernanke to speak to a crowd of nearly 1,200 individuals. Dr. Bernanke indicated that the economic models used at the Fed were little better than random. Yet many organizations make allocation decisions based on value forecasts from experts that have, on average, less expertise and/or resources than the Fed. In 1929, the Harvard Economic Society declared that a depression was "outside the range of probability." Nearly eighty years later, 97 percent of economists surveyed by the Federal Reserve Bank of Philadelphia in November 2007 forecasted a positive growth rate for 2008;[4] nearly two-thirds of professional forecasters expected growth above 2.0 percent.

There are those, though, whose predictions turn out to be correct; let's consider the forecasts of four individuals credited with having foreseen the economic and financial crisis of 2007–2009.[5]

Between mid-2006 and early 2007, Med Jones of the International Institute of Management published a series of papers in which he argued that economic growth was less sustainable than commonly thought, fueled by household debt and a housing bubble. He specifically indicated that the highly rated mortgage-backed securities promoted by Wall Street were in fact very high-risk securities. In March 2007, he indicated to Reuters that "if people started to think there may be a lot of bankruptcies (in the subprime lending market), then you're going to see the stock market sell off." In early 2009, he also accurately predicted the bottom of the recession and anticipated modest recoveries in late 2010 and early 2011.

At a meeting of the International Monetary Fund in September 2006, the economist Nouriel Roubini laid out arguments for a recession in the United States deeper than that of 2001. In his full testimony, he discussed the deep decline in housing resulting in a significant impact on consumers becoming a contagion to financial institutions and other market players.

Peter Schiff of Euro Pacific Capital, while on Fox news in December 2006, indicated that the U.S. economy was not strong, and as a result the housing market would decline significantly and unemployment would rise. Three out of four of Schiff's fellow panelists on the program vehemently disagreed with him. In August 2007, a member of a similar panel referred to the subprime issue as minor; many agreed that the equity market was a buying opportunity, opposing Schiff.[6] Finally, Dean Baker of the Center for Economic and Policy Research also predicted a housing bubble.

In analyzing successful predictions made by experts, there are three significant issues. First, there are approximately 14,600 economists in the United States alone, plus other noneconomist forecasters. Observing that some of them foretold the crisis is not surprising. This is the same problem as the one we faced in chapter 3 when we wanted to distinguish skills from luck in fund managers' performance. Second, it is unclear if these forecasts provide an estimate of the depth of the crisis and its translation into quantitative predictions used for portfolio allocation.

Third and most importantly, with the exception of Med Jones, the three other forecasters lack unblemished forecasting records.

For example, Dean Baker made his first prediction of a housing correction in 2002, more than five years prior to the actual event. When housing prices peaked sometime in 2006, they were more than 50 percent above their 2002 level and nominal prices did not go below the 2002 level even at the worst of the housing crisis. We can conclude that the 2002 forecast was premature. Furthermore, Baker is the same economist that criticized Bill Clinton in 1999 for proposing a fix for Social Security, arguing that the projected insolvency was extremely unlikely. He called it a phony crisis and projected surpluses for Social Security of $150 billion by 2008 (in 1999 dollars). Social Security has been running a deficit since 2010, which will only grow unless policy changes are implemented.[7]

Similarly, Nouriel Roubini predicted recessions in 2004, 2005, 2006, and 2007. He also failed to predict a worldwide recession at the time. In his own words: "I do not expect a global recession, I think it is going to be a slowdown." He again forecasted recession for 2011 and 2013, in addition to these post-crisis statements: "U.S. stocks will fall and the government will nationalize more banks as the economy contracts through the end of 2009" (March 2009),[8] "We're going into a recession based on my numbers" (August 2011),[9] "Whatever the Fed does now is too little too late" (September 2011),[10] "The worst is yet to come" (November 2012).[11]

Peter Schiff wrongly predicted post-crisis interest rates increasing, hyperinflation, the dollar dropping, gold nearing $5,000, and more. Since 2010, he has been forecasting some form of financial and economic collapse. His daily radio show, "The Peter Schiff Show," was broadcast from 2010 to 2014 to sixty-eight stations in thirty states and up to 50,000 listeners online. His website advertised six books, five of which have the word "crash" in their titles. It would be imprudent to point to his success while ignoring the many failures. Anyone forecasting a financial catastrophe will eventually be proven right. Statistically, such an event will happen again given a long enough horizon. However, a specific forecast is only useful to investors if accompanied by a reasonable timeline (such as being right in the next two years, not in the next ten years), and the forecasters should only be given credibility after the fact if the trigger was properly identified by the forecaster (such as being right for the right reason).

Tetlock classifies experts in two groups: "Foxes," who have a more balanced approach and see shades of gray, and "Hedgehogs," who do not allow for the possibility of being wrong. Foxes are cautious and less exciting. Hedgehogs, meanwhile, are confident entertainers. Those who rise to fame may be better at marketing themselves than at making forecasts. As investors during the 2007–2008 crisis, we would have needed to sift through the thousands of forecasters to determine the worth of the individual forecasts of our chosen experts.

Issues of sample size also affect forecasting accuracy. There have been twenty-two recessions in the United States since 1900, according to the National Bureau of Economic Research. A *New York Times* article in October 2011 indicates that the Economic Cycle Research Institute, a private forecasting firm created by the late economist Geoffrey H. Moore, had correctly called all recessions over the last fifteen years, or a total of two events for the United States. The article states: "In the institute's view, the United States, which is struggling to recover from the last downturn, is lurching into a new one. . . . If the United States isn't already in a recession now it's about to enter one." An eventual recession is inevitable, but has not happened yet (as of mid-2016). This is not to discount the ECRI, but to point to the need for a better sample size to render a definitive decision.[12]

Prakash Loungani of the International Monetary Fund gave a damning assessment:[13] only two of sixty recessions worldwide during the 1990s were predicted a year ahead of time and only one-third by seven months. Recessions are usually forecasted upon reaching the cusp of disaster. Furthermore, the larger issue for asset managers is not only whether economists and other forecasters fail to anticipate a recession, but also if they do call a recession that does not occur.

Overconfidence has negative effects on forecasting, as with investing. Ohio State University professor Itzhak Ben-David and Duke University professors John Graham and Campbell Harvey analyze responses of chief financial officers (CFOs) of major American corporations to a quarterly survey run by Duke University since 2001.[14] CFOs are asked their expectations for the return of the S&P 500 Index for the next year, as well as their 10 percent lower bound and 90 percent upper bound, which should allow for only a 20 percent probability that the actual returns would fall outside of the estimated range. By definition, overconfident individuals would provide tight lower and upper estimates and would likely be wrong more than 20 percent of the time. In reality, market returns remained *outside* the set limits 64 percent of the time.

These observations are entirely consistent with the work of Glaser, Langer, and Weber on overconfidence. In an experiment, they asked a group of professional traders and a group of students to complete three tasks:[15]

- Answer knowledge questions (ten questions concerning general knowledge and ten questions concerning economics and finance knowledge).
- Make fifteen stock market forecasts.
- Predict trends in artificially generated charts. This approach neutralizes the "expertise" advantages that experts may have over nonexperts.

This experiment also required experts and students to provide a lower and upper estimate that had a 90 percent probability of including the right answer. All results confirmed overconfidence among experts and nonexperts. Interestingly, although traders are more confident than students, they are not more accurate. We can conclude that knowledge impacts confidence levels but does not necessarily improve accuracy.

Our choices in forecasting methodology also work to illustrate the difficulties of making accurate predictions. Dukes, Peng, and English surveyed the methodologies used by research analysts to make their investment recommendations.[16] Did they use the theory-grounded dividend discount model (DDM) or another method? About 35 percent of analysts admitted using this approach, though it was rarely the primary decision driver. The favorite approach (77 percent) was some form of price-earning (PE) multiple applied to an earnings forecast. Though users of the DDM approach will use longer time horizons to forecast earnings and dividends (five years), those that rely on a PE multiple approach use a short-term horizon (one or two years), an implementation ill-equipped to deal with regression to the mean.

Montier evaluated the performance of portfolios over a long period by the ranking deciles of historical and forecasted PEs and found no material difference.[17] He found that analysts who prefer stocks with greater earning growth expectations see historical earnings momentum as the most important determinant of future earnings momentum. Almost invariably, their top quintile of highest future earnings growth stocks is composed of securities having the highest historical five-year growth in earnings. This again illustrates that the concept of reversion to the mean is ignored. Montier reported that when analysts forecast earnings twelve months ahead, they were wrong by an average of 45 percent,[18] concluding that most analysts simply follow trends.

The PE forecast approach is a shortcut methodology because a PE level incorporates implicit assumptions about earnings growth, inflation, and risk. However, although the DDM approach is conceptually superior, its application is challenging. The estimated fundamental valuation of a security derived from a DDM approach is extremely sensitive to the assumptions made about the growth rate in earnings and the discount rate. For example, let's assume an analyst believes earnings will grow by 8 percent per year for five years and then by 5 percent afterward. Let's also assume the risk premium on this security is 4 percent and the long-term risk-free rate is also 4 percent. What would be the approximate valuation difference if we were to instead assume a growth rate of 10 percent for the initial five years and a risk premium of 3.5 percent? The price valuation difference would be more than 31 percent. Hence analysts prefer the PE forecast approach because it is far easier to anchor the forecasted PE on the current PE and to limit the earnings forecast horizon to a few years than to meet all the requirements of a DDM implementation. However, these forecasts based on short-term considerations have limited long-term value to investors.

We Know Less Than We Are Willing to Admit

Forecasting is difficult, and our failures lie in our desire to prefer one form of forecasting over another, use of improper forecasting horizons, and overconfidence in forecast accuracy. Many investors have unreasonable expectations: they aim for positive and stable excess performance at short horizons.

Asset prices are influenced by fundamental factors and noise. However, the shorter the horizon, the greater the ratio of irrelevant noise to relevant information. What most significantly determines the pattern of returns on the S&P 500 at a one-second horizon? Is it noise or is it fundamental factors? What if we were to ask the same question for a horizon of ten seconds, a day, a month, a year, or ten years? After all, luck, which is performance attributed to noise, fades over time.

There is simply too much noise and volatility around expected returns at short horizons to showcase our predictive abilities.

The daily volatility of the S&P 500 since 1980 is 1.11 percent. Observing a 2 percent move on a given day does not represent even a two standard deviation move in the market. Thus, most of the time, such movement does not require a unique explanation other than simply the confounding effects of market participants' actions during the day. We should not expect to necessarily find a rational explanation for the security price movements that we observe on a daily basis.

Yet financial news looks to experts for daily interpretations of market movements, and sometimes the same explanation can be used to justify opposite market movements, such as:

> The equity market rose today because several indicators show improving prospects for economic growth.
>
> The equity markets declined today because investors are concerned that improvement in some key indicators for economic growth may lead to rising interest rates and a less accommodating monetary policy.

Do market commentators know what is good for financial markets and the economy? Let's consider the global market correction that occurred after Ben Bernanke made several announcements on June 19, 2013, concerning a hypothetical scenario for ending the unprecedented liquidity injection after the liquidity crisis.

> the Committee reaffirmed its expectation that the current exceptionally low range for the funds rate will be appropriate at least as long as the unemployment rate remains above 6 and 1/2 percent so long as inflation and inflation expectations remain well-behaved in the senses described in the FOMC's statement . . . assuming that inflation is near our objective at that time, as expected, a decline in the unemployment rate to 6 and 1/2 percent would not lead automatically to an increase in the federal

funds rate target, but rather would indicate only that it was appropriate for the Committee to consider whether the broader economic outlook justified such an increase.

Importantly, as our statement notes, the Committee expects a considerable interval of time to pass between when the Committee will cease adding accommodation through asset purchases and the time when the Committee will begin to reduce accommodation by moving the federal funds rate target toward more normal levels.

Although the Committee left the pace of purchases unchanged at today's meeting, it has stated that it may vary the pace of purchases as economic conditions evolve. Any such change will reflect the incoming data and their implications for the outlook, as well as the cumulative progress made toward the Committee's objectives since the program began in September. Going forward, the economic outcomes that the Committee sees as most likely involve continuing gains in labor markets, supported by moderate growth that picks up over the next several quarters as the near-term restraint from fiscal policy and other headwinds diminish. We also see inflation moving back towards our two percent objective over time. If the incoming data are broadly consistent with this forecast, the Committee currently anticipates that it would be appropriate to moderate the monthly pace of purchases later this year; and if the subsequent data remain broadly aligned with our current expectations for the economy, we would continue to reduce the pace of purchases in measured steps through the first half of next year, ending purchases around midyear. In this scenario, when asset purchases ultimately come to an end, the unemployment rate would likely be in the vicinity of 7 percent, with solid economic growth supporting further job gains, a substantial improvement from the 8.1 percent unemployment rate that prevailed when the Committee announced this program.[19]

Here's a quick summary of the above transcript excerpt:

- *When* the unemployment rate is close to 6.5 percent (it was 7.6 percent at the time of the statement), the FOMC committee will determine whether or not circumstances dictate that the federal fund rate should increase.
- A fairly long period will be observed between the end of the asset purchase program and the increase in the federal fund rate.
- The committee made no change to the current asset purchase program.
- *If* inflation increases toward 2 percent and if the unemployment rate eases toward 7 percent, the asset purchase program may have been ended.

The market reacted badly to these statements. According to Paul Christopher, chief international strategist at Wells Fargo Advisors, "People aren't sure that the economy is well enough for the Fed to pull back.... The market is signaling to the Fed that we don't trust your assessment of the economy; we don't trust your assessment of inflation."[20] Ben Bernanke responded to doubts of this sort as such:

> If you draw the conclusion that I've just said that our policies, that our purchases will end in the middle of next year, you've drawn the wrong conclusion, because our purchases are tied to what happens in the economy.

In the end, the market reached a new high less than three weeks after the June 19 press conference. The asset purchase program was first reduced in December 2013 and ended in October 2014 as the unemployment rate declined more quickly than market participants or the Federal Reserve expected. The job gains in 2014 were the largest since 1999 and total employment surpassed the pre-crisis peak by 2.7 million.[21] At that time, inflation was inching toward 2 percent, but the larger than expected decline in energy and commodity prices put significant downward pressure on inflation in late 2014 and in 2015. The Fed eventually raised rates only in December 2015.

Consider the following interpretations from Bloomberg news on July 3, 2013: "U.S. stock-index futures remained lower after a private report showed companies added more jobs than economists forecast last month, fueling concern the Federal Reserve will begin to reduce monetary stimulus." A few hours later, the following comment was also made: "Stocks fell as turmoil in Egypt and political uncertainty in Portugal overshadowed better-than-estimated data on jobs growth and unemployment claims." By the end of the day they had come full circle with the following: "U.S. stocks rise as jobs reports offset Egypt, Portugal." The first statement makes the argument that equity markets declined because the risk of a reduction in monetary stimulus outweigh the benefits of better economic data, while the second and third statements support the argument that without the political uncertainty of Egypt and Portugal, the economic data would have supported rising equity markets. These contradictory statements raise another question: Why do we even ask for and read these comments? We should not assume that experts are correctly interpreting new information or even understanding its impact.

Overcoming Our Failures at Forecasting

Finucane and Gullion suggest that the key to a good decision process is "understanding information, integrating information in an internally consistent manner, identifying the relevance of information in a decision process, and inhibiting impulsive responding."[22]

There is evidence that we can improve our abilities to forecast both political and economic events. The work of Philip Tetlock on the inability of experts to forecast political events has had interesting consequences, leading the U.S. intelligence community to question if forecasts could be improved. Therefore in 2011, the Intelligence Advanced Research Projects Agency (IARPA) launched the ACE (Aggregate Contingent Estimation) program with an eye toward enhancing the accuracy, precision, and timeliness of intelligence forecasts across a variety of sectors.

The ACE program funded a 2011 tournament of five forecasting teams with fifteen thousand participants. Participants were asked to predict whether or not approximately two hundred events would occur, such as: Would Bashar al-Assad still be president of Syria by January 31, 2012? There was also a control group selected by the intelligence community. One of those teams, under the umbrella of the "Good Judgment Project," is based at the University of Pennsylvania and the University of California–Berkeley. The project is led by Phil Tetlock (a psychologist), Barbara Mellers (an expert on judgment and decision making), and Don Moore (an expert on overconfidence). In the first year, the Penn/Berkeley team far surpassed the competition. Their superiority was such that they were the only team that IARPA funded in the third year of the project.

According to Tetlock, "One thing that became very clear, especially after Gorbachev came to power and confounded the predictions of both liberals and conservatives, was that even though nobody predicted the direction that Gorbachev was taking the Soviet Union, virtually everybody after the fact had a compelling explanation for it. We seemed to be working in what one psychologist called an 'outcome irrelevant learning situation.'"[23]

In his opinion, few pundits are willing to change their minds in response to new evidence. They are also unable to outperform a random decision process. Experts rarely admit: "I was wrong"; rather, they claim: "I would have been right if not for . . ." The success of Tetlock's team can be partially attributed to a training model developed to teach forecasters how to choose relevant information and avoid bias. Some of the members did narrative thinking while others did probabilistic thinking. The latter were trained to turn hunches into probabilities and did better. For example, instead of basing their forecasts solely on their understanding of a situation, forecasters trained in probabilistic thinking would consider what has happened in other "similar" circumstances. Providing feedback of their performance was also helpful.

Tetlock found that among all the test subjects, the most successful predictions were made by a concentrated group of "super forecasters." Their personality traits, rather than any specialized knowledge, allowed them to make predictions that outperformed the accuracy of several of the world's intelligence services, despite forecasters lacking access to classified data. In the process of identifying better forecasters, hedgehogs disappeared and foxes thrived. Super forecasters are:

- Open-minded and more likely to look for information that challenges their own opinion,
- Trained in probabilistic reasoning and will collaborate with others to share information and discuss rationales,
- Update their predictions more often and spend more time challenging themselves.

There is a decisive parallel between political and financial/economic forecasting. Experts involved in financial and economic forecasts suffer from the same biases as political forecasters.

Few experts exceed the success of layperson forecasting. Michael Mauboussin discusses the conditions under which a crowd can predict with greater accuracy than experts.[24] He refers to the work of Scott Page, a social scientist who developed a simple understanding of collective decision making. According to Page, the collective error is equal to the average individual error minus the diversity of predictions. To illustrate his point, he used jelly beans in a jar as an example. X individuals guessed the number of jelly beans in the jar. Individuals were wrong by more than 60 percent, but all the individuals together were wrong by less than 3 percent. This concept is well known in financial circles; by aggregating all investors' opinions through price formation, financial markets effectively provide superior forecasts that are hard to beat with any non-price-based variable. There are always outliers, but from experiment to experiment, these are rarely the same individuals. The greatest danger lies in homogeny of opinions, when all agents think alike. Therefore we must not reject diversity, but embrace it.

Can Statistical Models Really Be Useful?

Can statistical models really outperform expert opinions and help to weed out conflicts of interests, marketing prowess, and distinguish luck from skills? Orley Ashenfelter, a Princeton economist, former editor of the *American Economic Review* and wine enthusiast, has published a number of papers since the late 1980s on the economics of wine, including a controversial equation designed to forecast the value of Bordeaux Grands Crus.[25] The equation takes just a few variables into account and explains more than 80 percent of the variations in prices: age of vintage, average temperature during growing season (April to September), amount of rain at harvest time (August), and amount of rain during previous winter (October to March).

Unsurprisingly, the Bordeaux equation was not welcomed among wine experts. For example, Robert Parker, the world's most influential wine critic, commented, "really a neanderthal way of looking at wine. It is so absurd as to be laughable." In short, "an absolute total sham."[26] Normally, the market value of the wine is not known until the wine is finally released and traded, which usually happens three years after the harvest. Because young Bordeaux Grands Crus need a maturation period of eight to ten years to be drinkable, a professional assessment is needed to determine the expected value of the wine.

However, the Bordeaux equation provides better estimates of future prices than experts. Storchmann presents the following example: "In 1983, Parker deemed the 1975 vintage in Pomerol and St. Emilion outstanding and awarded it 95 out of 100 points. He also added that the wines were too tannic to be drunk and should be stored for a long time (a sign of a great vintage). However, as these wines matured Parker dramatically adjusted his rating. In 1989, he awarded this very vintage only 88 points and recommended that the wine should be drunk immediately rather than stored. That is, within six years, Parker's 1975 vintage rating dropped from outstanding to below average. In contrast, the Bordeaux equation predicted the mediocre quality of this vintage already in 1975, immediately after the harvest." Overall, the equation predicted 83 percent of the variance in the price of mature Bordeaux red wines at auction.[27] Frank Prial of the *New York Times* wrote about the reasons wine experts attack the empirical approach:

> Two reasons. Some elements of the wine trade are angry because the Ashenfelter equation could be helpful in identifying lesser vintages they have promoted. . . . Second, more seriously, he is accused of relegating the whole wine-tasting mystique to a minor role. Supposedly, the sipping, spitting, sniffling and note-taking so dear to wine romantics have all been rendered obsolete by mathematics.[28]

Simple statistical models can also be useful in predicting expected financial returns. Of course, expert opinion is still needed if only to design better models. When we decide to invest in passive funds, the implementation of a portfolio is far from simple. We still need to determine which factors or asset classes to buy, a topic we will cover in the next two chapters. Similarly, for the statistical predictive model, we still need to decide which variables to use and how to control for statistical problems that will arise.

To understand our current abilities, it is important to know where we came from. At first, finance academics thought that returns were unpredictable. This is the fundamental claim made in the investment classic *A Random Walk Down Wall Street* by Princeton University professor Burton Malkiel. In such cases, the sophistication needed is at its lowest level: to forecast expected returns you only need to compute the historical average return that will be representative of future expected returns.

The 1980s saw the emergence of a ton of evidence of in-sample (i.e., after the fact) return predictability. An important and recurring theme of economic models that embed this predictability is that it is closely tied to the business cycle. For example, investors become more risk averse during recessions, leading to a higher risk premium.[29] Therefore recession forecasts also predict future higher average returns.

While these in-sample results already suffered from statistical biases,[30] an influential and award-winning study in the *Review of Financial Studies* in 2008 reveals that none of the predictors commonly used led to out-of-sample performance (i.e., when used before the facts) better than using the historical average return of an asset.[31]

In response, we have witnessed in the last few years a proliferation of statistical techniques that *do* lead to significant out-of-sample performance predictability. In a sense, the study mentioned previously helped to mobilize and organize the literature on these enhanced statistical techniques in finance. All of these methods deal to some extent with two crucial issues: model uncertainty (i.e., how is a predictor related to future returns?) and parameter instability (i.e., does the relation between a predictor and future returns change over time?).

These techniques are manifold. First, imposing economically sound restrictions leads to better out-of-sample forecasting performance. For example, economic intuition says risk premiums should be positive, and therefore negative statistical forecasts should be set to zero. Another example consists in averaging predictions made using a variety of simple predictive models, rather than using one complicated model with many predictors. These techniques cleverly rely on a diversification argument; it is better to diversify model risks than relying on one complex model that will overfit the data. Tetlock's team in the Good Judgment Project similarly designed algorithms to combine individual forecasts. The objective was to achieve a prediction accuracy that is on average better than the forecast of any single participant.

Some techniques go further by avoiding nearly any model estimation, for instance by fixing expected excess returns to the current dividend yield or payout yield. John Cochrane, in an excellent overview of the field of asset pricing, discusses how dividend yields predict expected returns in many markets.[32]

In the 1970s, when it was widely believed that equity returns could not be forecasted, a high dividend yield would have been interpreted as an indication of slower future dividend growth because higher dividends may indicate a low level of corporate investment. Alternatively, a low dividend yield would have been an indication of greater dividend growth. Therefore the dividend yield was believed to represent a view of future dividend growth, not future expected returns.

The data suggests the opposite. Higher dividend yields predict higher future excess returns and vice-versa. This pattern shows up in many markets:

- *Stocks*: higher dividend yields signal greater expected returns, not lower dividend growth.
- *Treasuries*: a rising yield curve signals greater one-year returns for long-term bonds, not higher future interest rates.
- *Bonds*: increasing credit spreads over time signal greater expected returns, not higher default probabilities.

- *Foreign exchange*: a positive interest rate spread signals greater expected returns, not exchange rate depreciation.
- *Sovereign debt*: high levels of sovereign or foreign debt signal low returns, not higher government or trade surpluses.
- *Housing*: high price/rent ratios signal low returns, not rising rents or prices that rise forever.[33]

These findings do explain why investors who use recent historical performance to make investment decisions usually do poorly. For example, increasing credit spreads lead to capital losses, which may cause some investors to exit the market, but make corporate bond investing more attractive.

Other powerful but more involved techniques extract predictive information from the whole cross-section of underlying assets. For an excellent treatment of these and other techniques, see the review by David Rapach of Saint-Louis University and Guofu Zhou from Washington University in the *Handbook of Economic Forecasting*.[34]

As an illustration, we provide the investment performance of an investor who invests only in the S&P 500 Index and short-term government bonds using only information that would have been available at each point in time. To guide his investment decision, he uses a combination of two of the above techniques. The return on a stock index can be written (in logarithms) as the sum of three return components: growth rate in the price-earnings multiple, growth rate in earnings, and growth rate of a simple transformation of the dividend-to-price ratio. These three components can be forecasted with simple quantities as follows: First, we can safely assume that price-earnings (PE) multiple cannot grow indefinitely in the long run. The collapse of PEs in the early 2000s following the technology bubble certainly illustrated this. We assume a constant PE and consequently set its growth rate to zero. Second, because growth rates in earnings are hard to predict, we use the twenty-year historical average. Third, we use the current dividend-to-price ratio as its forecast. Finally, following basic finance intuition, we expect investors to require positive excess returns on the market and set the forecast to zero if it happens to be negative.[35] We also do not allow for leverage.

Are expected return forecasts useful for investors? Table 4.1 suggests that they are. As we consider an investor who is only interested in maximizing his long-term compounded portfolio return,[36] the results in table 4.1 are easily interpretable. Each value represents the return for which the investor would be indifferent between the portfolio and a risk-free asset that pays this return each period. For example, the second-to-last column in the first row shows that an investor using the optimal forecast every month to rebalance his portfolio achieves an annualized geometric return of 8.72 percent. This favorably compares to 4.96 percent realized by an investor who uses the historical average available at each point in time (fourth column). The last column shows the difference between the two, which is 3.76 percent in this case. This difference can be understood as the maximum annual fee the investor would be willing to pay to obtain the expected return forecasts instead of using the historical averages. Finally, we also provide for comparison in the second and third columns the geometric return obtained by only investing in the short-term government bonds or only in the stock market. Again, using the optimal statistical forecasts is useful.

TABLE 4.1 Geometric return improvement in portfolio using expected return forecast (1950–2015)

Forecast and rebalancing frequency	Risk-free rate	100% invested in stock market	Optimal allocation based on historical average return	Optimal allocation based on forecasted expected return	Maximum fee an investor would be willing to pay to know forecast
Monthly	4.34%	5.88%	4.96%	8.72%	3.76%
Quarterly	4.34%	5.88%	4.78%	8.28%	3.50%
Annual	4.34%	5.88%	4.54%	6.94%	2.40%

As return predictability varies with the investment horizon, we also consider an investor who forecasts the stock market return and rebalances his portfolio each quarter (second row) and each year (last row). The usefulness of our expected return forecast is present at all horizons. Despite the simplicity of it all, most investors would not apply such a process because it would entail significant tracking error against the standard fixed equity/bond allocation benchmarks.

A common theme of most of these forecasting methodologies is that they imply simple predictive models. That simplicity trumps complexity is far from unique to expected return prediction. The great psychologist Paul Meehl reviewed the results of twenty studies that analyzed whether subjective predictions by trained professionals were more accurate than simple scoring systems.[37] The studies covered a wide range of forecast such as the grades of freshmen at the end of the school year, the likelihood of parole violations, of success in pilot training, etc. In all studies, the accuracy of experts was matched or surpassed by simple algorithms. Since then, the number of such similar studies has been expanded to forecasting medical issues (such as longevity of cancer patients), prospects of business success, winners of football games, etc. A meta-analysis of 136 research studies shows that mechanical predictions of human behaviors are equal or superior to clinical prediction methods for a wide range of circumstances (in 94 percent of such studies).[38]

That simple predictive models can be better or equivalent to subjective predictions of experts is sometimes difficult to accept. For example, Meehl indicates that some clinicians refer to statistical approaches as "mechanical, cut and dry, artificial, unreal, pseudoscientific, blind, etc.," while qualifying their method as "dynamic, global, meaningful, holistic, subtle, rich, etc." Asset managers using a discretionary approach sometimes make similar comments about quantitative and passive managers.

Even when a statistical approach can save lives, there is resistance to adopt it. Bloodstream infections in the United States kill

31,000 people a year. After the death of an eighteen-month-old infant at Johns Hopkins Hospital, Dr. Peter Pronovost designed a simple five-point checklist that has been very efficient at reducing, if not eliminating, such infections at Johns Hopkins.[39] Furthermore, the checklist was applied at more than one hundred ICUs in Michigan. The median infection rate at the typical ICU dropped from about 2.7 per catheter hour to zero after three months. The results were presented in the December 2006 issue of the *New England Journal of Medicine.* Yet despite the logic and simplicity of it all, the checklist is not widely accepted because, in the opinion of some, many physicians do not like being monitored by nurses or otherwise being forced to follow a checklist.

As reported by Meehl and Grove, "The human brain is an inefficient device for noticing, selecting, categorizing, recording, retaining, retrieving and manipulating information for inferential purpose."[40] Humans cannot assign optimal weights to variables (intuition only goes so far), even less so on a consistent basis. Second, according to Meehl, experts have a need to look clever, which can be achieved by relying on greater complexity. They feel they can override or outperform simple algorithms because they have more information. However, experts are also biased. They have their own agendas, personalities, misperceptions, dislikes, and career risks. They simply cannot accept the fact that in most cases simple statistical algorithms can outperform them. We should not try to shoot the messenger, deny our shortcomings, and pay higher fees for information that is nothing more than noise. To again quote Nassim Taleb: "Simplicity has been difficult to implement in life because it is against a certain brand of people who seek sophistication so they can justify their profession."[41]

Again, we stress that we should not conclude from all prior statements that experts are useless. We need experts to identify and understand the primary factors that impact a variable. Isolating substance from noise is the work of experts. Again, according to Meehl and Grove, "The dazzling achievements of Western post-Galilean science are attributable not to our having better brains than Aristotle or Aquinas but to the scientific method of accumulating knowledge," a process that is not well implemented in the financial industry at large, but may be found in specific knowledge-based firms. As mentioned in the introduction, we operate in an industry that resists accumulated knowledge when it threatens the existing business model.

Are We Any Good at Predicting Risk?

This chapter focused thus far on predicting expected values: expected economic growth, expected market returns, expected wine prices, etc. Expected returns are notoriously hard to predict, but it turns out that we are much better at predicting risk.

Consider volatility, which is a measure of the variability of returns around their expected values. Let's first examine why we can do a better job predicting volatility than expected returns. Figure 4.1 contains what financial econometricians call auto-correlation functions. Auto-correlations are measures of the degree of co-movements of returns with its own lags; for example, how today's return tends to be related to yesterday's return or to the daily return five days ago. If auto-correlations of returns were large, it would be easy to predict future returns from past movements alone. The black line shows the auto-correlations of daily returns of the S&P 500. Unfortunately, the black line shows that all auto-correlations are close to zero; it is difficult to infer a statistical relationship from past returns to predict future returns.

The dashed line shows the auto-correlations in absolute returns. Absolute daily returns are a proxy for volatility; indeed, a larger return in magnitude, regardless of whether it is positive or negative, is indicative of more variability. From this graph, we see that auto-correlation is positive and decays slowly as we increase the lag. Not only is the magnitude of today's return related to

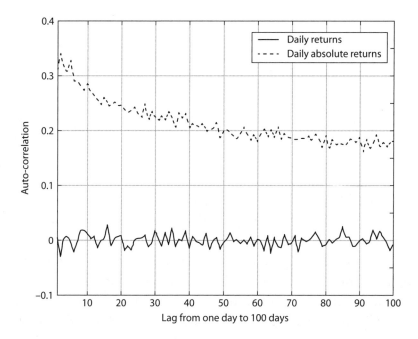

FIGURE 4.1 Auto-correlation functions of daily returns and absolute returns of the S&P 500 Index (1927–2015)

yesterday's, but also to five or twenty days ago. We usually refer to this phenomenon as volatility clustering: when risk is high in the markets, it tends to remain high.

As an illustration of the importance and of our ability to predict volatility, we provide in table 4.2 the investment performance of an investor who invests only in the S&P 500 Index and short-term government bonds. To control risk in his portfolio, he wishes to target at all times a volatility level of 10 percent, which is similar to what is obtained by investing in a balanced portfolio on average.

Every month, he uses the predicted volatility from a statistical model that is slightly more sophisticated than using a moving average of volatility.[42] The fourth column shows that the realized volatility by following this strategy from 1950 to 2015 would

TABLE 4.2 Investment performance of a portfolio invested in the S&P 500 that targets a 10 percent annual volatility (1950–2015)

	100% invested in stock market	Using historical market volatility	Using our volatility predictions
Average annualized return	7.35%	5.72%	6.44%
Annualized volatility	14.55%	6.92%	9.33%

have been 9.33 percent, pretty impressive given the simplicity of our volatility model and the fact that our sample period contains the crash of 1987 and the economic crisis of 2007–2009.

The targeted volatility compares favorably to the one obtained by using the historical volatility at each point of time as a forecast (6.92 percent) and to the one obtained by investing all the portfolio in the market (14.55 percent). Table 4.2 also shows that controlling volatility would have cost the investors only 0.91 percent (7.35 percent to 6.44 percent) in average returns. Figure 4.2 shows the time-varying volatility for the market and our portfolio that targets a 10 percent annual volatility.[43] Clearly the market experiences spikes in risk; the effect of the oil crisis in 1974, the market crash in 1987, and the financial crisis in 2008 are evident. Comparatively, our portfolio using our simple volatility predictions achieves a volatility that is close to 10 percent in all periods. Clearly we can forecast volatility.

We have used a model that relies solely on daily returns to make risk predictions. Of course, there exists a vast literature on models that better captures risk patterns in financial markets. In particular, a growing area of research concerns models that also use economic variables to forecast risk. Similar to expected returns, there exists a link between the business cycle and volatility. Much as expected return is high during recessions, volatility also tends to increase. Interested readers should

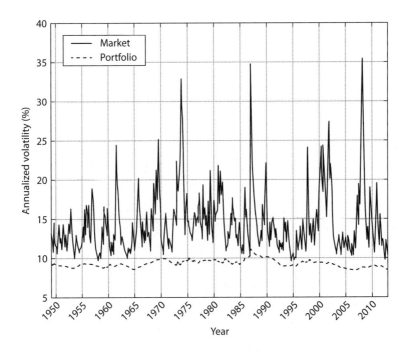

FIGURE 4.2 Time-varying volatility of the S&P 500 and the portfolio that targets a 10 percent annual volatility (1950–2015)

go to the excellent review in the *Handbook of the Economics of Finance* by Torben Andersen of Northwestern University, Tim Bollerslev of Duke University, Peter Christoffersen of the University of Toronto, and Francis Diebold of the University of Pennsylvania.

Again, we have provided an illustration based only on volatility. Risk is by no means only captured by volatility; a comprehensive portfolio management technique should take into account other measures of risk, especially measures of co-movements between different assets. The next two chapters will have more to say about risk measures. For an overview of models used for volatility and dependence, we suggest the excellent textbook *Elements of Financial Risk Management* by Peter Christoffersen.

Concluding Remarks

The major lesson from this chapter is that forecasts are unavoidable in asset management, but one should be aware that simplicity often trumps complexity. Just as it is important not to pay high management fees to a fund manager with no differentiating expertise, we should not pay a high price (e.g., with our time and attention) for subjective forecasts. In many cases, simple statistical techniques do lead to better results out-of-sample, and there has been tremendous progress in forecasting achievements in recent years. Chapters 5 and 6 will support this assertion.

Unfortunately, it has been our experience that many managers set their asset allocation strategies based on forecasts of events and explicit return forecasts (where the evidence of our ability to forecast is weaker), instead of building their strategy on the basis of risk forecasts (where the evidence of our ability to forecast is stronger). Obviously, it is a lot more interesting to discuss why we expect that Amazon will outperform Alphabet than to discuss how forecasting and managing volatility could improve compounded returns. The next two chapters will illustrate that it is unnecessary to do explicit return forecasts to outperform.

5

The Blueprint to Long-Term Performance

PORTFOLIO MANAGEMENT IS INHERENTLY a question of asset pricing, the field of economics concerned with understanding how financial asset prices are determined by investors' preference and the structure of financial markets. Understanding investors' preferences is crucial to portfolio management: it explains how prices are formed in financial markets and which risk factors F are compensating investors with positive average returns. It also highlights investor biases and errors that lead to mispriced assets. Simply put, understanding investors' preferences is paramount to portfolio management.

In chapter 4 we saw that as investors we need to understand the limitations of forecasting (especially at short horizons) and that successful forecasts of extreme events are often a one-time phenomenon. The poor track record of forecasters brought Howard Marks of Oaktree Capital to declare: "You can't predict but you can prepare."[1] What can be predicted to some extent are the characteristics of the probabilities of events.

A majority of investors prefer the most basic of these characteristics: higher average portfolio returns. To illustrate the source of average returns, our return equation from chapter 2 is once again helpful. From this equation, the return we can expect every period by investing in an asset is

$$E[R] = R_f + \alpha + \beta_m \times E[F_m] + \beta_2 \times E[F_2] + \ldots$$

where E represents the return R that is *expected*. The difference between E and the average return is a question of timing: E indicates what we expect the average return to be before it is realized, whereas the average return is the average of the realized returns after the fact. Clearly, when choosing a portfolio, we are forced to consider expected returns, not the yet-to-be-realized average returns or the historical returns. In this equation, we have the risk-free rate of return R_f, the mispricing α, the expected return of each factor $E[F]$, which is called a risk premium, and the asset's exposure to these factors β. The stock-specific shock ε is absent because it is purely an unpredictable (idiosyncratic) shock with an expected return of zero, and hence the average return unrelated to common risk factors is entirely captured by α. As a reminder, α can also be defined as the excess return attributed to a specific manager's skills and/or to his luck or the result of the portfolio exposure to risk factors that have yet to be properly identified and documented. In the end, it captures the mispricing of an asset.

This is not the whole story; another characteristic of the probabilities of events shows up on our radar: the risk of our portfolio. Again using our return equation, we can use the variance of returns, given by

$$Var[R] = Var[\beta_m \times F_m + \beta_2 \times F_2 + \ldots] + Var[\varepsilon],$$

to measure the risk of our investment. In a nutshell, the variance measures the variability of realized return around what is expected.

Just as we did in chapter 4, we often use its close parent the \
tility (or standard deviation), which is the square root of varia\
We prefer assets with lower variance because we are more certain
that realized returns will be close to what was expected. In this
equation, the mispricing α is absent because it is a constant and
has no risk (assuming you can identify its value). We use volatility
as a risk measure for our portfolio, but keep in mind that most of
the intuitive reasoning discussed shortly remains if we use a more
sophisticated measure of risk.

These last two equations are key to understanding why there
are three sources of sustainable long-term performance, whatever
the asset class, and that they are all related to a form of diversification: diversification of unrewarded risks, diversification of priced
sources of risk, and diversification of mispricing risk.

This chapter will show that these three forms of diversification
can be used to explain the long-term average return of most factor-based products (now referred to in the industry as smart beta
products) and fundamental management styles without assuming
that portfolio managers have any forecasting skill. Although forecasting can be useful, we need not explicitly forecast expected
returns to outperform. In this chapter we discuss each form of
diversification in detail. The more financially knowledgeable readers will notice that we are not reinventing anything here, but merely
presenting all sources of performance in a consistent framework.
Most investors are familiar with these sources of performance,
though they are usually presented in a less explicit fashion.

The field of asset pricing is often ignored when dealing with
portfolio management techniques, but these last two equations
show why it should not be. Before we explain why it matters so
much, let's consider how modern portfolio theory developed in
the 1950s and 1960s. The cornerstone of modern portfolio theory
comes from the work of Harry Markowitz, who showed how
to optimally combine assets in a portfolio to maximize reward
(expected returns) for a given level of risk (variance in this case).

The efficient frontier, which presents a set of optimal risk/return portfolios, is derived from this exercise. This is now considered the most basic portfolio management technique.

Asset pricing models go a step further than Markowitz did, without which any portfolio management technique is a lot less useful. Asset pricers ask what happens in equilibrium if all investors choose their portfolios using such a technique. Equilibrium is defined as a situation in which prices are set in the market so that there is no surplus or shortage of assets in the market (i.e., the market clears). The outcome of these models is the structure of expected returns, that is, which risk factors F are compensated and which mispricings α may persist in equilibrium. The structure of expected returns provides a roadmap to the investor for the optimal composition of his portfolio. Note the vicious circle: an asset pricing model shows how assets are priced and what the composition of your portfolio should be, but these models are derived from assumptions about investors' optimal portfolio allocation. Fortunately, we will not explore this issue further.

Hence we need some asset pricing models to understand what our return equation looks like in real life; this results in our optimal portfolio. The next section begins with a case that will lead to our first source of performance: diversification of unrewarded risk.

Diversification of Unrewarded Risk

Let's consider a case in which all stocks have the same expected return E[R]. When we combine these stocks in a portfolio, we necessarily get a portfolio that has the same expected return as any of its underlying stocks. However, the risk in our portfolio is a lot lower than the average risk of these stocks. We get the same level of reward E[R] but lower risk Var[R] because the idiosyncratic terms are diversified away; positive and negative asset-specific return shocks average out. Figure 5.1 illustrates this. Each month, we form a portfolio by randomly selecting among all U.S. stocks and computing the realized volatility from 1962 to 2012. By repeating this exercise numerously, say 100,000 times, we compute the average realized volatility of these portfolios. Figure 5.1 reports this average volatility on the vertical axis as a function of the number of stocks selected in the portfolios on the horizontal axis (from one to one hundred stocks). The black line compares the risk of value-weighted random portfolios to the value-weighted portfolio containing all stocks (dashed black line). Similarly, the gray line compares the risk of equally weighted random portfolios to the risk of the equally weighted portfolio of all stocks (dashed gray line).

Figure 5.1 shows the power of diversification in lowering our portfolio risk. But why should we care about risk if we get the

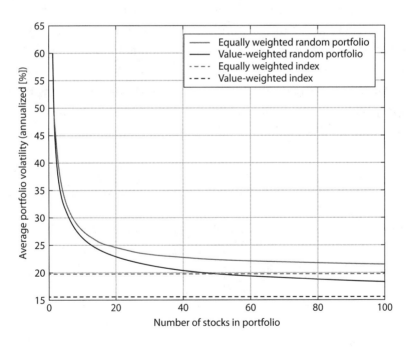

FIGURE 5.1 Average portfolio volatility of random portfolios of U.S. stocks held from 1962 to 2012

same expected return? The simplest way to show the importance of diversifying unrewarded risk is through the effect of compounding returns.

Let's consider the following scenarios. You invest $100 for twenty years and the average return of your portfolio is zero. If returns are certain, then twenty years gives you only the initial $100. However, what if the volatility of your portfolio returns was 1 percent? Or what if it was 5 percent? These are all scenarios in which the average return is 0 percent, but your final wealth would be drastically different in each case. Table 5.1 shows the expected growth rate of your portfolio in each scenario.

The average annual return is also called the arithmetic mean, while the effective annual return is called the geometric mean or compounded return. This very simple example illustrates how volatility amputates your portfolio growth rate and does so in a nonlinear way. Twice as much volatility will amputate performance by a factor of four and four times as much volatility by a factor of sixteen. Here is another example in which the average annual return is not 0 percent but the compounded return in nil. Let's assume you have a 50 percent loss followed by a 100 percent return. The average mean is 25 percent [(–50 percent + 100 percent) / 2], but your final wealth will be zero because a

TABLE 5.1 Expected geometric return over twenty years according to volatility scenarios

Volatility scenario	Average annual return (arithmetic mean)	Portfolio annual growth rate (geometric mean)
None	0%	0.00%
1%	0%	–0.01%
5%	0%	–0.13%
10%	0%	–0.50%
15%	0%	–1.13%
20%	0%	–2.00%

50 percent loss on your portfolio must be compensated by a 100 percent gain simply to get back to the initial level of wealth. Risk really does matter!

The geometric mean is always less than the average mean unless there is no risk (i.e., returns are identical in all periods). Bad risks (such as volatility and negative asymmetry—the fact that extreme negative returns may be more likely to be observed than positive extreme returns) amputate geometric returns. However, if we limit our concerns solely to volatility, the performance drain attributed to volatility alone is equal to one-half of the variance. The relation between the periodic expected returns (arithmetic mean) and geometric mean is the following:

$$\text{Geometric Mean} = E[R] - \text{Bad Risk} \cong E[R] - \tfrac{1}{2} \, Var[R].$$

This is not a forecast but a structural consequence of the impact of volatility on geometric returns. Hence we should diversify risks not associated with higher average (arithmetic) returns. Doing so is relatively easy. There exist portfolio solutions in the markets that aim to minimize risk and maximize diversification, some of which we will examine in the next chapter.

A common misconception is that diversification has a cost, that is, we get lower risk, but also lower returns. Diversification is all about having lower risk for a *given average periodic return.* When we diversify unrewarded risk, we remove the impact of the idiosyncratic terms' variance $Var[\varepsilon]$ on our portfolio variance (see the second equation in this chapter), which reduces the performance drag in the geometric mean expression. Diversification might not be a sexy issue, but it pays.

Commodities illustrate well the impact of more efficient diversification on the geometric mean. In 2006, two articles on the benefits of investing in commodities were published side by side in the same issue of the *Financial Analysts Journal.* Both articles analyzed the performance of investing in commodities between

1959 and 2004, yet their conclusions differed greatly. The first study concluded the geometric excess return on commodity futures was –0.5 percent on average, while the second study reported an average of +5.23 percent.

The answer to this puzzling fact can partly be found in how these averages are computed and how each methodology impacted volatility. The first study computed the geometric excess return of individual commodities and then calculated the average across all commodities.[2] Average geometric excess performance was –0.5 percent and the average volatility of each commodity was about 30 percent.

The second study created an equally weighted index of thirty-six commodities rebalanced monthly.[3] The portfolio volatility was only about 12.5 percent. Not only did the excess performance of commodities nearly match that of equity (5.65 percent), but risk was lower. In their opinion, commodities are an appealing asset class.

The average arithmetic return of all commodities and the average arithmetic return of an equally weighted portfolio of the same commodities are mathematically the same. Yet the spread in compounded returns between the two studies is nearly 5.75 percent. However, the previous equation states that volatility drains performance by half the variance. Assuming that the volatility of the average commodity is 30 percent and no rebalancing occurs, the performance drain from volatility would be as high as 4.5 percent (30%[2] / 2). However, if a portfolio has no more than 12.5 percent volatility, the performance drain is only 0.78 percent (12.5%[2] / 2). This factor alone explains nearly 3.75 percent of differential compounded return.

An equally weighted portfolio of commodities rebalanced monthly has much lower volatility than the average volatility of single commodities. This lower portfolio volatility is a result of their low cross-correlations, a measure of how much they co-move together, and of a portfolio assembly process that efficiently exploits these low correlations. Cross-correlations are as low as 15 to 20 percent on average, while they are more than three times as much for equities. Thus, the commodity asset class is incredibly heterogeneous and a perfect candidate for efficient diversification. Unlike equities that are subject to a dominant risk factor (the market), commodities related to energy, grains, livestock, metals, and precious metals have much less in common, which allows for the construction of portfolios having volatility as low as the 12.5 percent reported previously despite the high volatility of single commodities.

This example also conveys another message. When these articles were published, several investment advisors favored the study with the optimistic conclusion and recommended investing in commodities because they concluded that commodities offered a significant risk premium. However, the first study showed that these results were largely explained by the diversification benefits resulting from investing in an equally weighted portfolio, not necessarily by the extraction of risk premiums. Therefore these results could not be used to justify investing in commodities using a product that was not similarly diversified. For example, the S&P GSCI Index, with its heavy concentration in energy commodities, does not offer the same diversification benefits.

We are not saying, however, that maximizing geometric mean should be your objective. Rather, we are using it to illustrate the importance of reducing unrewarded risk in a portfolio. Investor preferences can lead to very different portfolios than that which maximizes the geometric mean. For example, the average annualized monthly excess returns and volatility of the U.S. stock market since 1971 are 6.47 percent and 15.79 percent, respectively. The allocation that maximizes the geometric mean is given by the ratio of the expected excess return divided by its variance.[4] In the case of our U.S. equity example, this ratio is 259 percent (6.47 percent over 15.79 percent squared). An investor would have to borrow 159 percent against his wealth. Clearly few of us would be comfortable with such leveraged investment. Furthermore, this conclusion assumes that volatility is stable. When volatility explodes in crisis time, the level of tolerable leverage usually is much less.

To ensure that we do not negatively impact the expected return of our portfolio, we must better understand what determines expected returns. Hence we are back to our emphasis on asset pricing, which is discussed in detail in the following section.

Diversification of Priced Sources of Risk

In the decade following Harry Markowitz's groundbreaking work, financial economists found the results should everyone follow his portfolio choice technique. In such a simple setup, called the capital asset pricing model (CAPM), the market portfolio F_m, in which all assets are weighted by their market value, arises naturally as the only source of positive average returns. According to this model, the market is the only risk factor and only the differences in exposure to risk factor β_m explains the difference in expected returns across portfolios or securities, such as Amazon having a greater market β_m than Walmart. This is an important theoretical finding with long-lasting impact. We have become accustomed to think in terms of this market portfolio. When we ask, "Did a fund manager beat the market?" we implicitly compare it to what should be done under the CAPM, that is, holding the market portfolio, and not to any other benchmark such as the equally weighted performance of all stocks. From our discussion in chapter 2 on the economics of active management, we remember that the market portfolio is the only portfolio that every investor can hold.

However, more than three decades' worth of academic research has shown that we live in a multifactor world. Financial assets' average returns are related to more than just the market factor. In the stock market, we have decades of evidence showing how value stocks, stocks that have a low price compared to their accounting value, tend to outperform growth stocks on average. In the currency market, forward contracts on currencies of countries with high interest rates tend to have higher returns than currencies with low national interest rates. Some factors are important in multiple markets, like momentum, the tendency of assets that have been recently trending up to have higher returns than those that have dropped. This factor appears to generate excess returns in all asset classes (equity, commodities, and currencies) and geographic regions. We will discuss this evidence later.

If average asset returns are related to several risk factors, we know that our portfolio should combine them in some way. By having a mix of all available risk factors, we will have less variable portfolio returns (the first component of variance in the second equation in this chapter is lower): when one factor is down, another might be up. For example, when small capitalization firms perform badly, value firms may perform well. Risk factors bring sources of average returns beyond the market risk premium, and bundling them up lowers total portfolio risk. Hence we should diversify these priced sources of systematic risk.

Let's first examine how traditional portfolios stand in terms of risk factor exposures. A typical balanced allocation puts 60 percent of a portfolio into the stock market and 40 percent in safe government bonds. Figure 5.2 shows the contribution to total portfolio risk of the stock allocation (black line), which is invested in the S&P 500 Index of U.S. stocks, and of the bond allocation (black dashed line), which is invested in a ten-year U.S. government bond. The portfolio risk (gray line) is measured here by the annualized volatility of the portfolio and is reported on the right-hand side axis as a reference.[5] Despite a 60 percent portfolio allocation, the contribution to total portfolio risk of the equity component is almost always higher than 80 percent, even higher than 100 percent during most years after 2000. The fact that the contribution of equity risk is always greater than 80 percent is attributed to the

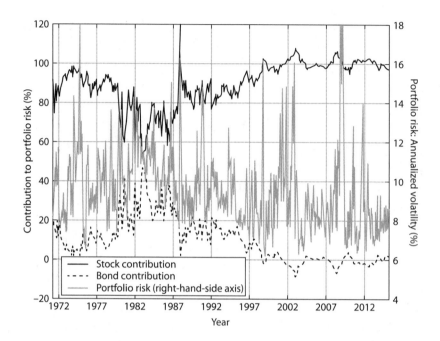

FIGURE 5.2 Contribution of the stock market and government bonds to a 60/40 portfolio's risk

much greater volatility of equity versus that of fixed income, even in normal times. But the observation that this contribution can be greater than 100 percent is attributed to specific periods in which equity risk is significant and correlation between equity and fixed income is negative. Several aspects contributed to this negative correlation. Fixed income acted as a safe haven, monetary policy favored fixed income assets in turbulent periods, and many large players, specifically pension funds, increased the duration of their fixed-income portfolio component. Hence the total portfolio risk is overwhelmingly driven by the equity allocation.

But this is an analysis based on asset classes (stocks versus bonds). Asset pricing models generally provide optimal portfolios based on risk factors, not asset classes. Asset classes are bundles of factors. Ang has an intuitive explanation for risk factors: risk factors are to asset classes what nutrients are to different foods—a balanced diet seeks to offer the appropriate mix of nutrients and should be tailored to individual needs. His argument is that investors should determine how much exposure their portfolio should have to specific risk factors and what appropriate mix of assets will deliver that exposure. This approach has the advantage of ensuring that the investor's portfolio diversification reflects the investor's desired risk exposures and may reduce the exposure to dominant risk factors, like the market. For example, many investors may not realize that some asset components (like emerging market bonds) are very sensitive to equity market risk and may have more exposure to equity risk than they believe.

Therefore let's analyze our 60/40 portfolio in terms of risk factor exposures. A total of five risk factors will be considered. First, we use the market factor defined as the excess return (above the risk-free rate) on the market portfolio of all U.S. stocks (the risk factor F_m should be the value-weighted portfolio of all available stocks, not an index of large capitalization stocks like the S&P 500). Then we use three other risk factors that are supported by tremendous empirical evidence: a size factor that buys small capitalization companies and sells large capitalization companies, a value factor that buys value stocks and sells growth stocks, and a momentum factor that buys stocks with high previous annual return and sells stocks with low previous annual returns. Finally, we include a risk factor used for government bonds, which is the return on a long-term bond minus the return on a short-term bond. Hence all factors are defined as long-short portfolios, even the market factor that is short the risk-free rate. We limit our analyses to these primary factors for simplicity.

Figure 5.3 shows the factor exposures through time of the 60/40 portfolio.[6] First, the exposure to the whole stock market hovers around 60 percent and the exposure to the size factor is around –10 percent, which indicates that the portfolio has negative sensitivity to smaller capitalization stocks. The negative sensitivity to

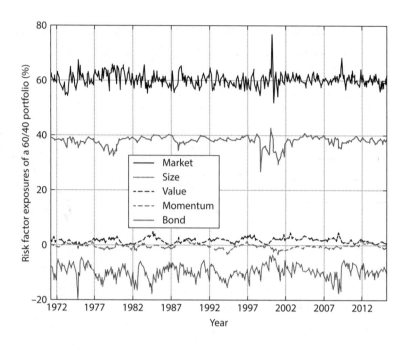

FIGURE 5.3 Exposures to risk factors of a 60/40 stock/bond portfolio

the size factor is not surprising. The market factor is built from all available U.S. stocks, while our portfolio is only invested in large capitalization U.S. stocks, those within the S&P 500. The S&P 500 has a large capitalization bias when compared to the overall equity market. Therefore to explain the performance of the S&P 500 Index, we need to buy the whole stock market (go long our market factor) and sell short small capitalization stocks (our size factor). Similarly, the bond allocation is captured by a 40 percent allocation to the bond risk factor. None of these results are unexpected.

Less appealing are the very low allocations to the value and momentum factors. If these are genuine risk factors for which investors receive compensation in the form of a risk premium, an investor interested in maximizing the risk/return profile of his portfolio should allocate to these risk factors. However, a standard 60/40 allocation based on the S&P 500 Index and the ten-year government bond is simply not designed to deliver a balanced exposure to all factors.

Figure 5.4 shows the comparative performance of our 60/40 portfolio and a portfolio in which we adopt an equal allocation to each of the above five factors (20 percent each), a very naïve but often efficient allocation implementation. Because factors are represented by long-short portfolios, the performance also incorporates the return of risk-free security.

The cumulative performance underlines the importance of factor diversification: for very similar average returns (9.57 percent versus 9.53 percent), we get a much lower risk (annual volatility of 9.96 percent versus 4.77 percent). Hence the terminal value of the equally weighted factor portfolio is greater, implying a greater

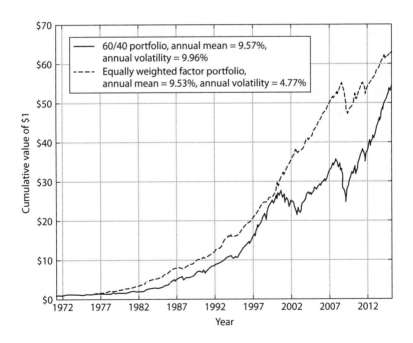

FIGURE 5.4 Cumulative performance of a 60/40 portfolio and an equally weighted portfolio of risk factors

geometric return despite a similar average return. Remember our first source of performance: lower volatility for the same level of expected returns results in higher long-term compounded returns.

Two caveats are worth noting at this point. First, we assume that investors can invest directly into these risk factors. However, in real life, these involve many stock positions, both long and short, and potentially high transaction costs. Chapter 6 deals with how to implement such improved portfolios in practice, either using portfolios of single securities or factor replicating exchange-traded funds. Second, we assume a prior knowledge of an equally weighted allocation providing good results. Equal weights are used for simplicity here, and a closer look at optimal allocations in practice will be explored in chapter 6.

Must we simply better balance risk factors in our portfolio for optimal performance? Of course not. Investors have hetero-geneous preferences. Risk factors exist because some investors have a reason to avoid the systematic risk to which these factors are exposed. For example, risk-averse investors avoid stocks with high exposure to the market β_m as these stocks are more likely to fall with the market. Stocks with higher β_m should theoretically have higher average returns to compensate investors for bearing this risk. What about the economic explanation for other risk factors? The jury is still out. It is not that we do not know what causes these effects. Rather, we have too many competing eco-nomic stories. For example, value stocks fall a lot at the onset of economic recessions,[7] value firms face higher cost when dis-investing assets in place during recessions,[8] are more exposed to labor income risk,[9] may not have the flexibility to adjust to com-petitive changes without facing significant cost commitments and losses on outdated infrastructure, etc. A potential explanation for momentum is the fact that it is exposed to severe downside risk; the momentum factor in the U.S. stock market lost more than 70 percent between July and August 1932 and more than 55 percent from February to September 2009!

Hence common risk factors exist because they expose you to some form of systematic risk that cannot be diversified away. In figure 5.4, we obtained a better performance only because we examined the problem through the lens of an investor who wants to optimize average returns and reduce volatility. Keep in mind that we collectively own the market. If, for example, we adopt an allocation different from the market portfolio by overweighting value stocks, it means that somebody else is willing to take the opposite bet. Of course, some of these risk premiums could also be due to irrational mistakes investors make, but we will cover that possibility in a later section.

Because of the many risk factors proposed by academics and practitioners, a proper understanding of the economic forces at work is crucial. To ensure that you include a genuine risk factor in your portfolio that will give you sustainable excess performance, it should have a valid economic basis for existence, should be easily measurable (impact from a once-in-a-century natural disaster, for example, would be hard to properly analyze), and should be supported by strong out-of-sample empirical results. We come back to this point later in the chapter.

A Closer Look at Empirically Motivated Risk Factors

Empirically motivated factors are factors that are supported by strong out-of-sample empirical results but were not necessarily derived from a well-defined economic model. Size, value, and momentum are examples of such factors.

The fact that small stocks or value stocks that look underpriced compared to their accounting value subsequently have high returns might seem like a tautology. Of course cheap stocks would have higher returns! But the surprising fact is not that small or value stocks tend to have higher average returns, rather it is that their average return is not explained by their exposure β_m to the market portfolio. In fact, none of this should be surprising at all. It simply shows that average returns are related to more risk factors than only the market.

As in the case of value, it is not the metric usually used to express value (the book value-to-market price ratio) per se that is priced. If all one had to do was to look up a stock's price on *Yahoo Finance* and its book value in the company's latest financial statement, compute the ratio, and invest in companies with a high book-to-price ratio, everyone would do it. This in turn would bid up the prices of value stocks and put downward pressure on the prices of growth stocks until the anomalously high average returns would disappear. The fact that this does not happen indicates that value is a proxy for a source of systematic risk (i.e., is exposed to this risk) that asset pricers have not yet fully understood. Hence investors expect to be compensated to support this risk.

To get a better sense of empirically motivated factors such as size and value, remember that according to basic finance theory the price of an asset should equal expected discounted cash-flows:

$$\text{Price} = \Sigma \text{ (Expected cash flow at time t)} / (1 + E[R])^t.$$

In this equation, which we will call our price equation, the left side is the price observed in the market and the right side is the sum of all the cash flows received in future periods discounted to the present time. Following basic finance intuition, we discount future cash flow (the numerator) because cash in the future is less valuable than the same amount today. Because these cash flows are uncertain, we discount them using a higher or lower expected return (the denominator) depending on their riskiness.

Is this a new model compared to our return equation? Not really. Imagine you are planning on selling a stock in the next period. In this case, the only expected cash flow that matters for you is the expected market price and possible dividend payout at the time you are going to sell. The expected return in the denominator is the same as in our return equation at the beginning of this chapter. We are simply expressing the relation in terms of cash flows instead of returns. Once you consider all future cash flows, the denominator becomes a measure of the long-term average expected return. Put simply, buying an asset at $100 and expecting to sell it for $105 is the same as having an expected return of 5 percent. This price equation is a general representation of market prices, just as the return equation was a representation of realized return. Both are generic and do not rely on any model.

Now consider two companies with the same expected cash flows for all future periods (the same numerator on the right side of our price equation). If one has a smaller price, expected returns (the denominator on the right side) must be higher. Similarly, if both companies also have the same accounting book value and we divide both sides of our price equation by their book value, a lower price-to-book ratio on the left side implies a higher expected return in the denominator on the right side.

In this example, the size and price-to-book value ratios of these companies become signals or proxies for expected returns required by investors. But if we could truly control for factors that explain expected return, this relation would disappear. In other words, expected return should be entirely explained by the true risk factors, not characteristics like size or price-to-book. The fact that we still find a relation empirically and that this relation is persistent simply means that we have yet to find the right model for expected returns E[R]. This intuition is not surprising for academics and has been understood for more than twenty years.[10]

Hence many empirically motivated variables, such as value and momentum, find much more empirical success than theoretically motivated factors, such as downside risk and liquidity risk. This is also not surprising. For example, downside risk has the ability to explain momentum profits, and liquidity risk has the ability to explain the size effect. Both measures are motivated by an economic model, that is, we understand why they should be the right risk factors in real life. But they are not completely successful at explaining the momentum and size effects because downside risk and liquidity risk are hard to measure empirically. Readily available measures such as the size of a company or its return over the last year do not suffer from such measurement issues and can therefore perform better empirically.

Diversification of Mispricing Risk

Let's now discuss our third and final form of diversification. At its peak in the summer of 2000, Nortel Network, the former Canadian electronic and communication giant, traded at 125 times earnings and represented more than 30 percent of the Canadian equity index. To put this figure into perspective, its market capitalization was 40 percent of Canada's GDP! But by the end of 2009, Nortel had filed for bankruptcy.

An interesting consequence of securities that are apparently overvalued is that they will also have among the biggest weighting in a capitalization-weighted index. Because the price of a security influences the total market value of a firm, if the security is relatively overpriced (compared to other securities in the index), it will have more weight than it deserves in the index. The reverse is also true. At its peak, Nortel accounted for a significant portion of the Canadian market index simply because the stock was expensive. When the price of Nortel collapsed, indexed investors lost significantly, not only because of the substantial price decline, but also because it had the highest weighting in the index. Investors lost significantly on a large portfolio allocation.

Prices are not always equal to their fundamental values. The holy grail of investing consists of identifying which securities are undervalued and which are overpriced. We want to overweight the former and underweight or simply avoid the latter.

However, when buying a security, the only information we know with certainty is its market price.

Think back to our discussion in chapter 2: markets should be inefficient (assets should offer a non-zero α) to entice active investors to look for them and make prices more efficient. We can capture this intuition by adding a mispricing on the right side of our price equation:

$$\text{Price} = \Sigma \left[(\text{Expected cash flow at time t}) / (1 + E[R])^t \right] + \text{Mispricing.}$$

Of course, the mispricing comes from the presence of a non-zero α in the expected return in the denominator, but we write it as a separate term for expositional simplicity. Why is α referred to as a mispricing? Consider two stocks that have the same exposures βs to all risk factors F. If their αs are not equal, they must be relatively mispriced because we could buy the one with the highest α, short sell the other, and obtain a positive average return without any systematic risk. At first sight, picking stocks with high α appears to be a very profitable endeavor.

Just as understanding why some investors shun some source of systematic risk and give rise to the existence of risk premiums, it is crucial to understand the origin of a mispricing. Conceptually, mispricing is literally free money; an appropriately diversified portfolio with a positive α provides positive returns every period with no risk! Simply to exist implies that other investors behave irrationally and do not pick up this free money. For such mispricing to disappear, all we need is one rational investor in the market who is not constrained in taking advantage of these arbitrage opportunities. He could buy positive α assets, hedge away the risk factor exposures by short selling negative α assets, and obtain positive average returns free of systematic risk. Such trading should put pressure on prices until these αs disappear, effectively arbitraging away mispricings.

However, there are plenty of reasons why these mispricings persist in financial markets. We have already discussed the need for the existence of α to entice active investors to invest in research. Another important reason is *limits to arbitrage*, which are all those frictions that prevent smart investors from picking up this free return (difficulty in shorting stocks or sustaining a significant short position over a long period, leverage constraints, limited liquidity, policies that restrict large investors from holding specific assets such as lower grade bonds or sectors linked to higher carbon emissions, etc.). Thus, even if we believed in 2014 or early 2015 that the Shanghai Shenzhen CSI 300 Index was grossly overvalued, and even if it were easy to implement a short position, it would have required significant staying power and courage to bet against a horde of retail investors in a country where the middle class numbers over 300 million and is growing by the millions, creating new demand for equity. Similarly, much courage was required in 1999 to significantly underweight technology stocks.

A quick look at the expressions at the beginning of the chapter for average return and variance reveals a key fact: maximizing the average return on a portfolio can be done by investing in high α assets, but doing so exposes your portfolio to more concentrated asset-specific risk Var[ε], which increases the overall risk of your portfolio. For example, at one extreme, if you believe you can pick high α stocks, you should keep in mind that you still face a tradeoff between this source of return and the negative impact of the higher portfolio variance on your geometric return. Put simply, if you determine that Apple Inc. has a positive α, you shouldn't bet it all on Apple. There is a combination of Apple shares and risk factors that has both the same average return and lower risk.

At the other extreme, if you believe you have absolutely no expertise in identifying high α stocks, there are no reasons to hold anything else than a combination of risk factors. Any other portfolio exposed to single stocks would have higher risk without higher average return.

There is a middle ground. If you instead form a well-diversified portfolio that tends to overweight high α assets (i.e., undervalued assets) or underweight low α assets (i.e., overvalued assets) or both, you are letting diversification eliminate the impact of asset-specific random shocks while still taking advantage of mispricings. The trick is to identify variables that could be correlated with underpricing, or at least not correlated with mispricing, and form a portfolio based on these measures.

For example, Research Affiliates' Fundamental Indexes (RAFI) avoid using market capitalizations as a weighting mechanism because of their sensitivity to mispricings. Their intuition is simple: an overpriced stock is more likely to be overweighted in a market capitalization–weighted index because the stock price itself is a component used to determine its weight in the index. Instead, they use accounting variables that are less sensitive to mispricing to weight their portfolio solutions, variables such as cash flows, sales, book value, and dividends paid. For example, the amount of sales of GM and Apple tell us very little about the mispricing of these two securities, and so the correlation of sales to mispricing should be low. Other weighting methodologies also lead to a lower correlation between portfolio weights and overpricing, such as using equal weights or simply using a moving average over time of market capitalizations.

Nevertheless, the intuition that mispricing imposes a performance drag on market capitalization–weighted portfolios crucially depends on the correlation between market prices and mispricings and the very existence of this performance drag is contested.[11] Also, if prices are on average equal to their fundamental values, a fact on which fundamental indexes rely to declare that prices eventually revert to fundamental values, returns of securities that tend to be more dramatically mispriced will offer a mispricing risk premium.[12] Overall, we need to understand that things are not as simple as just using metrics other than prices to form a portfolio. Fortunately, the methodologies that emphasize risk factors and the ones that focus on the effect of mispricings in the market are not drastically different. The next section discusses this point further.

Risk Premium, Mispricing . . . Why Do We Even Care?

It is hard for most of us to precisely identify mispricings, so taking advantage of mispricings boils down to forming a portfolio based on a variable that we hope is correlated with underpricing or at least is uncorrelated with it. This sounds suspiciously like the way we constructed risk factors in a previous section. So what is the real difference between a risk premium and a mispricing-immune portfolio?

They differ greatly in terms of economics, but not drastically in practice. A risk premium is a rational compensation for exposing yourself to a systematic risk. Investors on the other side of the trade have other constraints and preferences and are happy to lose this risk premium. Mispricing is the result of irrationality in markets and can create average returns with no associated risk. These mispricings may persist because investor psychology does not correct itself, but most importantly because some financial frictions prevent it from being fully arbitraged away.

This economic difference underlies their potential sustainability. If you believe you are exposing yourself to a risk factor, you should understand the economic motive for investors to take the opposite bet and give you some average returns. If you believe you are taking advantage of a mispricing, you should understand the friction in the market that prevents it from being arbitraged away.

Most importantly for investors, the solutions offered to attenuate the impact of mispricings on market indexes are aligned with the objective of including risk factors other than the market portfolio. As specified earlier, RAFI uses weights based on accounting variables' relative values across companies, another approach uses moving averages of market capitalizations to form weights, and an extreme solution consists of forming an equally weighted portfolio. In each case, we implicitly diminish the role of the market capitalization–weighted portfolio and load up on other factors. As such, forming a portfolio whose weights are correlated with underpricings is in line with the objective of building factor-replicating portfolios. In one case, we wish to attenuate the impact of behavioral biases on the performance of market capitalization–weighted indexes. In the other, we want to deviate from a pure market index–based portfolio and include other risk factors. The question of whether one variable is related to risk or not is of lesser importance for investors who are well-diversified across mispricing- and factor-replicating portfolios. Although the underlying philosophies of factor-building portfolios and mispricing-neutral portfolios are different, the impact on portfolio structure can be similar.

Mispricings only appear as mispricings *within the current financial paradigm.* As finance academics develop a better understanding of investor preferences and the inner workings of financial markets, it is possible that sources of returns once perceived as being created by irrationality in financial markets will no longer appear as mispricings. John Cochrane, an economist and professor at the University of Chicago Booth School of Business, points out that "the line between recent 'exotic preferences' and 'behavioral finance' is so blurred that it describes academic politics better than anything substantive."[13]

Let's Go Fishing for Factors!

So we can bundle up different risk factors to get a better portfolio. We examined U.S. stock risk factors in a previous section, but evidence is also available for other asset classes: value and momentum are profitable in U.S. and international stocks, international equity indices, government bonds, commodity futures,

·ency forwards,[14] the interest rate–based factor in cur-
~y market,[15] or the term structure slope factors in the bond
and commodity markets.

But here's the tricky part. The risk factors that we can find by
solving an economic model of the world are usually harder to
measure and don't perform as well. We can instead go fishing
for factors, analyze the data, and find what looks like priced risk
factors. But finding such empirically motivated factors boils down
to data mining and does not necessarily guarantee future average returns (spoiler alert: calling it *smart beta* does not change
a thing). A recent study headed by Duke University's Campbell
Harvey lists more than three hundred risk factors that have been
studied in the literature.[16] They propose statistical means of dealing with different issues; for instance, the fact that the same datas-
ets (such as U.S. stocks) have been tortured in multiple studies and
that only good results are published and unsuccessful ones are not.
Many risk factors do not pass a sufficiently high statistical hurdle.

Consider the lifecycle of an academic publication that discov-
ers a new risk factor. The authors of a paper run their empirical
analysis on a sample period that ends as recently as data availability permits. They present their results in conferences and submit
their paper for peer review at a journal. This second step may
take several years, during which anonymous experts critique the
paper and ask for further analysis or changes. The paper may
even go through the rounds at several journals until an editor
decides to publish it. Investors become aware of the paper's findings either before or after publication. A recent *Journal of Finance*
paper studies the effect of publication on newly discovered factors.[17] They study ninety-seven variables that have been shown to
forecast stock returns in academic publications. One possibility
is that results are pure data mining, which means that average
returns after the publication's sample period are no more likely to
be positive than negative. They find that average returns fall on
average by 26 percent, which suggests that some data mining may

be at work. The overall average decline after publication is 58 percent, indicating that a newly discovered factor's average return is halved once results are published. Return predictability is far from disappearing completely, but we need to be careful in selecting factors and in adjusting our expectations of future average return. In our professional careers, we have witnessed this phenomenon many times. A few years ago, an institutional investor asked us why we did not incorporate a new but debated factor in our portfolio management process. We replied that at the time there was insufficient empirical and conceptual evidence of its validity, but this did not deter their insistence that we should incorporate it.

In chapter 6, we'll look at case studies involving different portfolio solutions, focusing on widely used and empirically supported factors such as market, value, momentum, and carry. Readers interested in knowing more about factors should consider the excellent textbook treatment in Antti Ilmanen's *Expected Returns*.

Concluding Remarks

We simply do not know what the market will throw at us in the future. Therefore it makes sense to adopt an approach that integrates all sources of long-term excess performance. The critical issue is to determine what comprises expected returns and to focus on proper risk management. The three forms of diversification cover each aspect of the return equation: the appropriate exposure β to risk factors F, the efficient diversification of idiosyncratic risks ε, and mispricings α. Explicit return forecasts, such as whether stocks would outperform bonds in a given year, were not needed in this framework.

It is also very useful that our blueprint to long-term performance is not asset class specific. The three forms of diversification are not equity-centric, but can theoretically be applied to all public market asset classes, whether equity, commodities, currencies,

ncome. They can also be implemented within the alloca-
... process of a balanced portfolio. It does not mean that each
form of diversification will have the same beneficial impact on all
portfolios and in all regions. The potential for diversification of
mispricings, factors, or unrewarded risks will vary depending on
the structural nature of asset classes and markets and their efficiency and also on the portfolio constraints imposed by investors,
but the principles remain valid in all situations. They form the
basis for general investment principles and can be used to explain
the expected long-term return structure of almost any portfolio.
This framework helps us isolate which products and/or managers
are more likely to be part of the winning group.

There is also another aspect that requires further clarification.
The framework we have discussed applies to traditional managers and alternative managers alike. The same portfolio structural
qualities that can be used to explain much of the performance of
traditional managers can also be used to explain that of a large
segment of the hedge fund industry. The fact that hedge funds
operate with very permissive investment policies does not change
this conclusion. Hence it makes little sense to pay five times as
much in fees for a hedge fund manager than for a benchmark
agnostic factor-based long-only manager. Investors can obtain
much of the factor exposure provided by hedge funds through
their traditional mandates at a lower cost.

Now that we have whetted our appetite, we turn in the next
chapter to the practical implementation of better portfolios. We
have not yet discussed the impact of investment policy decisions.
It is obvious that these decisions, such as choosing whether or not
leverage, shorting, and derivatives should be allowed, do impact
the potential for superior risk-adjusted returns and our ability to
implement them. But they do not impact our understanding of the
sources of this potential. The next chapter discusses how these
investments and constraints impact portfolio selection in practice.

6

Building Better Portfolios

IN THIS CHAPTER, WE focus on what it all comes down to: building better portfolios and analyzing their performance. We consider two investors with different constraints: an institutional investor who is relatively unconstrained in the type of assets he can trade and allocations he can adopt, and a retail investor who is relatively more constrained.

We build portfolios based on the blueprint for long-term performance set out in chapter 5. Our objective is twofold. Of course, we examine the ability of an investor to invest by himself and generate value. However, the results of this chapter are also useful because of the benchmarks they provide. These benchmarks should be used when making a decision to hire a fund manager, listen to a professional forecaster, or even determine the efficiency limits of what can be achieved in portfolio management. Indeed, once we understand how and why we can build better portfolios, we can still delegate the management of our portfolio, but our expectations should have correspondingly increased and our tolerance for high fees declined.

The main conclusion of chapter 5 was that we should hold a combination of well-diversified risk factors. This next section discusses how to construct such risk factors. Then we will consider how an institution like a mutual or a hedge fund can significantly increase its risk-adjusted performance by adequately combining these risk factors into a stock portfolio.

We'll then examine different portfolio solutions offered in the market and show how each one combines risk factors intelligently. Our discussion of a portfolio of U.S. equities will be useful to examine the relative merits of alternative weighting mechanisms that are being offered to investors.

We repeat our exercise by examining the performance of a portfolio that invests in risk factors across different asset classes: U.S. and international stocks, government bonds, commodities, and currencies. These portfolios would likely be appropriate for a sophisticated institution with the internal ability to implement an investment strategy, which requires programming skills, standard databases, and execution capabilities.

We next turn to our second category of investors. We have in mind as a good representation of this group a retail investor investing his personal savings; an investor with basic knowledge of Excel, who has limited time to spend on managing his portfolio and who is more restricted in terms of investment universe and borrowing limit. This investor faces higher transaction costs than an institution, which will force him to invest in exchange traded funds. He also cannot use any funding, which prevents him from shorting securities or using leverage. We'll use this investor to explore whether or not to hedge currency risk, but our conclusions will also apply to institutional investors.

These examples will take advantage of the current investment and statistical literature. We show the impact of using robust statistical predictions of expected returns across asset classes and using risk models with varying degree of sophistication.

How Can We Build a Specific Risk Fac

Remember that a factor is a portfolio that is compensated with positive average returns in equilibrium. Relatively few of these exist. The objective is to build a portfolio:

- that is well diversified such that it is not unfavorably impacted by idiosyncratic risk *(diversification of unrewarded risk)* and
- that is either linked to a source of systematic risk (to achieve *diversification of priced sources of risk*) or that exploits a source of persistent mispricing in financial markets (to achieve *diversification of mispricing risk*),
- all while picking up as little as possible of other factors.[1]

This is no small feat, especially in markets in which there are thousands of securities to consider. There are many possible answers to this problem.

One route often taken to create a factor is to build both a well-diversified portfolio of securities that have a high exposure to the targeted variable *and* a well-diversified portfolio of securities that have a low exposure to the targeted variable, then to buy the first portfolio and short sell the second. For example, the small-minus-big (SMB) market capitalization factor[2] is obtained by separating all U.S. stocks using the median size as well as the thirtieth and seventieth percentiles of book-to-market ratios of stocks listed on the New York Stock Exchange to form six different market capitalization–weighted portfolios. The first portfolio contains small capitalization and low book-to-market ratios; the second portfolio contains small capitalization and medium book-to-market ratios; etc. The resulting size factor is the average performance of the three portfolios with small stocks minus the average performance of the portfolios with large stocks.

The ingenuity of these long-short portfolios comes from the fact that we are isolating the desired exposure to a factor while largely neutralizing the effect of other factors. First, unless there is a strong relation between size and market beta (there is not), we obtain a portfolio with a close-to-zero exposure to the market portfolio by buying one and shorting the other. Indeed, the average exposure of the longs gets canceled by the average exposure of the shorts. A similar argument holds for the exposure to the value factor. By taking the average performance of a portfolio of small stocks with low, medium, and high book-to-market ratios and doing the same for the portfolio of large stocks, we cancel the average exposure to the value factor when computing the long-short portfolio. Another advantage of this construction methodology is that each of the six portfolios are value-weighted, which prevents small illiquid stocks from overly impacting the performance of the risk factor.

Another construction method based on ranks is sometimes used by Andrea Frazzini of AQR Capital Management and Lasse Pedersen of AQR, NYU Stern School of Business, and Copenhagen Business School. The idea is to rank all securities based on their value of the variable associated with the factor. For example, out of one thousand securities, the stock with the highest book-to-market ratio gets a rank of one thousand, and the stock with the lowest ratio gets a rank of one. To obtain a long-short portfolio, we subtract the median rank (500.5) and rescale all weights such that the factor is one dollar long and one dollar short. The security with the highest value metric therefore receives a weight of 0.40 percent and the stock with the lowest metric has a weight of –0.40 percent. All other stocks have weights in between these two extremes, depending on their book-to-market ratio. There are pros and cons to using rank-based factors. Let's first consider the pros:

- We avoid choosing thresholds like the median or other percentiles to separate stocks (a stock with a value of a variable on the verge may switch between long and short with small fluctuations);
- Rank-based factors can be more suited to building factors in asset classes where the number of assets is low, for example commodities and currencies;
- Threshold-based factors (as described previously), by sorting on both size and book-to-market ratio, are hard to generalize when one wants to use more than three factors (triple or quadruple sorts quickly become problematic). Rank-based factors are immune to this complexity because they rely on sorting on only one variable.

On the other hand, a single sort may not be as efficient to neutralize the impact of other factors. For example, by sorting simply on size we may indirectly load on other factors. Furthermore, a ranking approach may attribute significantly larger weightings to smaller securities that are much greater in number than larger securities despite the effect of the ranking mechanism.

In the next two sections, we investigate portfolios of U.S. equities to illustrate the concept and use of factors in portfolio design. To conduct our experiments, we rely on the database of factors built by AQR Capital Management and regularly updated online.[3] We take a moment to underline this contribution, which is too important to relegate to an endnote. Researchers who post their data online allow others to expand on their work. Assuming the data construction is adequate, making data available to all ensures that new discoveries can be validated faster by homogenizing our data (we avoid debating whether new facts are due to differences in data construction). Legions of researchers have benefited from data sources like those found on Ken French's website, and now on AQR's data library. Though both are useful, we mainly use AQR's data library because it contains the daily and monthly factor returns for a wide variety of countries, regions, and asset classes. In almost all cases in this chapter, we use data that can be found online, such that interested readers can replicate our results.[4]

An Institutional Portfolio of U.S. Equities

Let's begin with a first example: the U.S. stock market. Table 6.1 shows summary statistics of the historical performance of factors constructed from all available U.S. stocks from 1931 to 2015.

Our first factor is the market portfolio built from all available U.S. stocks weighted by their market capitalization minus the one-month Treasury bill rate. Panel A in table 6.1 shows that this factor has offered investors an annualized excess return of 7.92 percent for a volatility of 18.28 percent, giving a Sharpe ratio of 0.43 (0.0792/0.1828). In panel C, we see the same summary statistics for the period from 1951 to 2015 because this is the period that will be used later when implementing a portfolio of these risk factors (we use the first twenty years of returns to make a decision on the first portfolio allocation). Over the post–World War II period, the market portfolio has offered an average return of 7.12 percent and a volatility of 14.88 percent.

Our second and third factors are related to size (the market capitalization of a company) and value (the ratio of accounting book value to market value of a company). Why are these factors important? These are the star examples of empirically motivated risk factors as discussed in chapter 5. In papers in the *Journal of Finance* in 1992 and in the *Journal of Financial Economics* in 1993, Gene Fama and Ken French (yes, them again!) showed that many of the factors that had been used in the literature in the 1980s to explain U.S. stock returns could be summarized through the size and value effects. This three-factor model has since become a staple in the empirical asset pricing literature. More recently,

TABLE 6.1 Historical performance of U.S. factors

	Market	Size	Value	Momentum	Low-beta
Panel A: Historical performance, 1931–2015					
Annualized average excess returns (%)	7.92	3.50	4.95	7.65	8.22
Annualized volatility (%)	18.28	10.83	14.89	15.99	10.78
Annualized Sharpe ratio	0.43	0.32	0.33	0.48	0.76
Skewness	0.23	3.03	3.33	−3.26	−0.75
Panel B: Cross-correlations, 1931–2015					
Market		0.33	0.31	−0.33	−0.11
Size			0.30	−0.23	−0.03
Value				−0.69	−0.13
Momentum					0.28
Panel C: Historical performance, 1951–2015					
Annualized average excess returns (%)	7.12	1.71	3.14	9.01	9.65
Annualized volatility (%)	14.88	8.99	11.07	13.27	10.39
Annualized Sharpe ratio	0.48	0.19	0.28	0.68	0.93
Skewness	−0.55	0.60	0.92	−1.68	−0.59
Panel D: Cross-correlations, 1951–2015					
Market		0.27	−0.11	−0.12	−0.10
Size			0.05	−0.19	−0.02
Value				−0.64	0.12
Momentum					0.18

the same authors have proposed a five-factor model in which the three original factors are augmented with a profitability factor and an investment factor. Highly profitable firms and firms that invest less tend to have higher returns than firms with low profitability and a high investment rate. As of now, there is much debate in the academic world as to the most appropriate measure and economic explanations for these effects; we will let the debates continue evolving before considering them.

These factors are constructed as discussed previously: by separating all stocks using percentiles of market capitalization and book-to-market and taking a long position in the portfolios with small stocks (high book-to-market) and short selling the portfolios with large stocks (low book-to-market).

The size and value factors provided an annualized average return (already in excess of the risk-free rate because these are long-short portfolios) of 3.50 percent and 4.95 percent with volatilities of 10.83 percent and 14.89 percent, yielding Sharpe ratios of 0.32 and 0.33, respectively. Performances were slightly less favorable over the shorter period from 1951 to 2015, with Sharpe ratios of 0.19 and 0.28, respectively.

We consider momentum as our fourth factor. Momentum is constructed by first sorting stocks on size and then on returns over the last twelve months, skipping the last month to avoid the return reversal effect, which results in six market capitalization–weighted portfolios (small and loser stocks, small and stable stocks, etc.). The last month is skipped because research has found that momentum strategies based on short horizons of one-week to one-month returns deliver contrarian profits over the next one week to one month. The factor is the average return of winner portfolios minus the average return of loser portfolios. Momentum is another empirically motivated factor that has had tremendous success, mainly because it offers superior risk-adjusted performance. During the years from 1951 to 2015, it has offered 9.01 percent annual excess return on average, higher than the market's 7.12 percent, while having a lower annual volatility of 13.27 percent.

The final factor we consider is the low-minus-high beta factor. In a 2014 *Journal of Financial Economics* paper, Andrea Frazzini and Lasse Pedersen expand on the ideas in a publication from 1972 by Fischer Black (of the Black and Scholes option-pricing formula). They show that investors looking for higher returns but constrained by the amount of borrowing they can take will bid up the prices of risky high-beta stocks. In basic models in which investors are financially unconstrained, investors looking for higher returns can borrow to lever up the market portfolio. But in settings in which investors cannot borrow or can only borrow up to a certain limit, they are forced to buy riskier securities and shun safer ones. Their actions may make low-beta stocks more attractive in terms of risk-adjusted returns, and a factor that goes long low-beta stocks and that shorts high-beta stocks will offer positive risk-adjusted returns.

The low-beta factor has delivered a whopping 0.76 Sharpe ratio from 1931 to 2015 and 0.93 from 1951 to 2015, easily beating the performance of all other factors. We include the low-beta factor because it is a perfect example of what we should be looking for: a factor motivated by a simple, straightforward economic theory and supported by overwhelming empirical evidence. Frazzini and Pedersen illustrate the profitability of the low-minus-high beta in international equity markets, government and corporate bond markets, commodities, and currencies.

Of course, there are other factors supported by theory, for example, liquidity risk[5] and systematic return asymmetry.[6] But as we discussed in chapter 5, many of these economically motivated factors are hard to measure and construct. Another reason why we focus on market, value, and momentum is that these factors are relatively easy to apply in different markets, a feature that will be useful later in this chapter when we examine multi-asset class portfolios.

All of these factors are also appealing because of the low correlations they have with the market index, as well as among themselves. Indeed, the cross-correlations reported in panels B and D for the two sample periods range from −0.33 to +0.33, meaning that they do not co-move much together. This is close to the Holy Grail in investing: assets that deliver positive risk-adjusted returns, and each tends to zig when others zag!

The only exception is the value-momentum pair whose low correlation is a mechanical result of their own construction. The value metric is constructed by dividing the accounting book value by the most recent market capitalization (e.g., dividing book value from December 2014 by the July 2015 market capitalization to obtain the August 2015 value ratio) instead of the market capitalization at the same point in time as the accounting information (e.g., dividing book value from December 2014 by the same month market capitalization to obtain the August 2015 value ratio).[7] Hence a stock whose price has recently fallen will often end up in the long portion of the value factor and the short portfolio of the momentum factor, and a negative correlation will ensue.

This may seem too good to be true and to a certain extent it is. The cross-correlations in panels B and D are imperfect measures of dependence, meaning they hide extreme risks. These factors do not co-move much together in normal times, but they can be highly correlated during extreme periods,[8] a feature that was highlighted during the so-called Quant meltdown in August 2007.

These factors by themselves may also present other forms of risk. The last row in panels A and C presents the sample skewness of monthly factor returns. Skewness is a measure of the asymmetry of returns; negative values indicate that an extreme negative return is more likely than an extreme positive return. Similarly, a positive skewness means that an asset is more likely to shoot up than to plummet. Table 6.1 shows that both the momentum and the low-beta factors exhibit strong and negative skewness. Therefore we can understand these factors' high Sharpe ratios as a compensation for downside risk: they offer high returns on average because they sometimes crash dramatically, an aspect that investors tend to downplay when investing in normal times.

These factors are not always profitable. Historical performances are graphically presented in figure 6.1, which shows the rolling ten-year geometric returns (annualized) for each factor.

Each point represents the average compounded return an investor would have experienced over the previous ten years for each factor. For example, in the mid-1970s, investors in the equity market would realize an overall return close to zero over the last ten years. Also, an investor who had invested in the stock market ten years before the 2008 financial crisis and who was forced to sell at that moment would realize a negative return. Clearly, there is no factor that dominates all the time. One notable fact: it appears that the market portfolio has dominated all other factors for the ten years leading to 2015, a situation not seen since the late 1950s.

This also explains why market-neutral products (those products that seek to eliminate market risk but remain exposed to other factors) have performed relatively poorly in recent years when compared to standard long-only balanced products. Furthermore, products that eliminate the market factor fall into the alternative industry segment, a sector known for its high fees. Hence from a fee point of view it is cheaper to invest in multifactor products that integrate the market factor than it is to invest in traditional products with an overlay of factor-based market-neutral strategies. Furthermore, because the correlation of the market factor to other factors is low, some portfolio construction efficiency is lost if all factors are not managed jointly within an integrated portfolio management process.

Figure 6.1 also serves as a warning against our natural tendency to favor strategies that have performed well recently while shunning ones that have not. It would have taken a considerable amount of confidence to tilt your portfolio toward value stocks in the early 1960s or in the late 1990s. But value has been profitable in many markets and over a long period of time. There will always be short-term differences in factor profitability. The least we can do is focus on factors for which we understand the economic motivation (we understand why somebody else is taking the other side of the trade) and that are supported by vast empirical evidence.

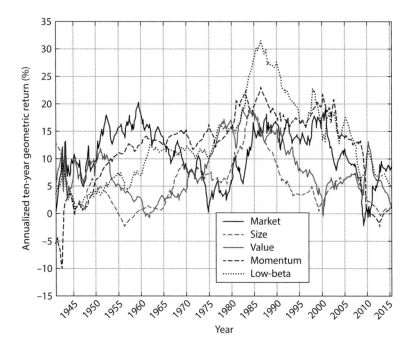

FIGURE 6.1 Ten-year rolling annualized geometric returns for U.S. equity factors

Now that we have established our investment universe of factors, we need to decide how to allocate among them.

Are Optimal Allocations Useful at All?

How do we allocate among assets? First, remember the importance of asset pricing theory in portfolio management. Investors form their portfolios according to their investment objectives and constraints, and prices form in financial markets. The result is a set of risk factors that offers positive average returns and possible mispricings to take advantage of.

We use the same asset allocation techniques to allocate among the risk factors that academics use to derive investors' allocations and equilibrium prices. The only difference here is that we abstract from equilibrium consideration: we take the set of priced risk factors as given and try to combine them optimally.

Different investors have different preferences. A retail investor may want to accumulate wealth over a long horizon for his retirement and might prefer to hedge his labor income risk; a portfolio that provides a positive return and is liquid if the economy sours and he loses his job would be highly appealing to him. A pension fund will focus on maintaining its ability to fulfill pension promises made to retirees that are often linked to inflation. Mutual funds may focus on outperforming a benchmark index; hedge funds, their absolute performance. The latter two also care about outperforming their peers. In contrast, central banks may intervene in financial markets to influence interest rates and exchange rates, but care less about risk-adjusted performance.

All portfolio management techniques follow the same mold. They maximize a preference metric, subject to financial constraints and a model for how financial asset returns are generated. Portfolio management techniques range from the very simple to the very complicated, depending on the complexity of preferences, constraints, and asset return dynamics.

We begin with the simplest case, one that aims at maximizing the Sharpe ratio. We want to maximize the expected return of our portfolio (financial reward) while minimizing the amount of portfolio volatility (financial risk) with no consideration for anything else. While we use this as a starting point, this is not that far from what is done in reality. John Cochrane of the University of Chicago Booth School of Business notes, "Much of the money management industry amounts to selling one or another attempted solution to estimating and computing [the optimal Sharpe ratio portfolio], at fees commensurate with the challenge of the problem."[9]

The ideal allocation for an investor who wants to optimize his portfolio's Sharpe ratio and faces no constraints is well known and available in closed form.[10] The optimal weight of an asset increases with its expected excess return, decreases with its volatility and cross-correlation to other assets. But this closed form solution is far from useful. In practice, investors face different allocation constraints, which means that the allocations will usually be obtained through a numerical optimization.

For example, imagine that you manage a U.S. equity fund and you rebalance your portfolio once a quarter by investing in the five U.S. equity factors. To capture the fact that volatilities and correlations in financial markets tend to change over time, you use a moving average of sample volatilities and correlations. At this point, we consider only one layer of sophistication: you use an exponentially weighted average to compute daily volatilities and correlations.[11] First, an exponentially weighted average places more weight on recent data, which is convenient because volatilities and correlations tend to be better forecasted by their recent levels than by longer averages. Second, you use daily returns even if your investment horizon is quarterly because having more returns for a given period gives you more precise risk estimates. This is in sharp contrast to estimating expected returns, in which having higher frequency returns does not give you more precise forecasts.[12]

Judging performances from historical simulations is always a difficult issue, and we need to work hard to make our experiment as realistic as possible. Every quarter, we use only the past histories of daily returns that would have been available at that point in time (for example, using daily returns up to June 30, 2015, to compute the allocation used on July 1, 2015). We also assume that factors are traded. But they involve thousands of stock positions. Of course, there is a high degree of netting out when they are combined (a stock's short position in a factor may be canceled by its long position in another factor). We present here the results based on the factor returns, but we acknowledge that in reality an institutional investor would implement a sampling technique that would limit the number of stock positions, the number of transactions, or both.

We compare the performance of this fund with that of a 100 percent allocation to the market portfolio and limit the fund's volatility to the benchmark's level of volatility, which is around 15 percent over the whole period. For expected returns, we set all expected excess returns to the same level, removing the knowledge that one factor would perform better than another. This is equivalent to using a minimum variance portfolio, a point we will return to later.

The second column in table 6.2 shows the performance of the stock market portfolio as a benchmark, and the third column reports on our optimal allocation without use of leverage. The Sharpe ratio almost triples from 0.48 to 1.40. This is rather spectacular, especially given that the optimal weights reported in figure 6.2 do not vary that much. In fact, the optimal allocation

TABLE 6.2 Performance of optimal portfolios of U.S. factors (1951–2015)

	U.S. Equity Market Index	Optimal portfolio without leverage	Optimal portfolio with leverage	Optimal portfolio without leverage and with tracking error constraint at 5%
Annualized average excess return (%)	7.16	6.29	12.30	6.98
Annualized volatility (%)	14.89	4.48	8.72	10.57
Annualized Sharpe ratio	0.48	1.40	1.41	0.66
Skewness	−0.55	−0.75	−0.79	−0.69
Annualized tracking error (%)		12.78	12.17	4.93

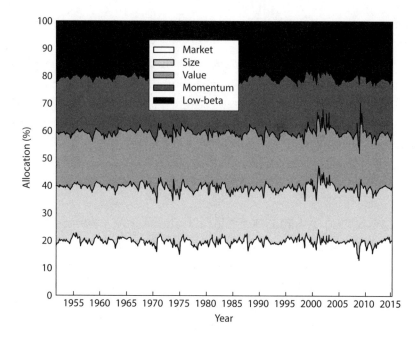

FIGURE 6.2 Allocation to U.S. equity risk factors in a Sharpe optimal portfolio

resembles the equally weighted portfolio that we used as an example in chapter 5. This is not surprising, given a few factors: we have constrained the expected returns to be equal, the volatilities are not that different, and cross-correlations are low, in which case the two portfolios are close to each other.

The Sharpe ratio is definitely impressive, but the average return is still slightly lower than the market portfolio. The increase in Sharpe ratio comes from a dramatic decrease in volatility due to diversification benefits. But what if you want more risk and more return? The fourth column shows the results by running the same portfolio with a limit of 200 percent on the portfolio weights. This allows a timid amount of leverage, especially given what sophisticated institutions can take on in real life.[13] In this case, the portfolio achieves an average return of 12.30 percent versus

7.16 percent for the market portfolio, and a volatility of 8.72 percent versus 14.89 percent.

The efficiency of diversification across factors leads to portfolios with high Sharpe ratios but low volatility. This explains why managers of efficient factor-based products (such as equal risk premia products) will often use leverage. Their investors want a product with a high Sharpe ratio but still want the greater expected nominal returns that can only be obtained from leverage. However, it does not mean that significantly greater portfolio efficiency cannot be obtained without using leverage.

Table 6.2 also reports that the optimal portfolios have lower skewness than the market portfolio. This is bad; we want positive skewness, or at least not too negative skewness. How should we assess if going from –0.55 to –0.75 is acceptable? The answer is that we cannot. Our portfolio management technique is based on maximizing the Sharpe ratio as a preference metric, not on maximizing skewness. Achieving lower or even higher skewness with the optimal portfolio is done purely by chance. We therefore cannot use it as an assessment of our portfolio quality.

This is a subtle but important point. How we evaluate portfolios has to be in line with our preference metric. Here we aimed to maximize the Sharpe ratio, and this objective was achieved. If we also care about the asymmetry in returns, our preference metric should be different. Plenty of other ratios, such as the Sortino ratio, take into account asymmetry. In a similar vein, if an investor maximizes the Sortino ratio when deciding on his portfolio allocation, he should look at the realized Sortino ratio, not the Sharpe ratio or any other performance metrics, to decide whether he has been successful.

It is a crucial point to keep in mind when evaluating alternative portfolio solutions. For example, let's say you find that an equally weighted allocation has realized a higher Sharpe ratio than the portfolio that tried to maximize it. You need to understand *why* it led to better performance or the results may have been obtained purely by chance and are not likely to be repeated. An equally weighted portfolio could be better, for instance, if expected returns, volatilities, and correlations are so hard to estimate that you are better off statistically to assume that they are all equal, in which case the equal weight allocation is the optimal Sharpe ratio allocation.

Even if there is netting out of long and short stock position when we allocate between the five factors, the optimal portfolio considered so far may involve some short selling of individual stocks. Further, the last line in table 6.2 reports the annualized tracking error, which is the volatility of the return differential between the portfolio and a benchmark, which in this case is the U.S. equity market index. A higher value implies that a large difference in return, positive or negative, is more likely to be experienced on any given month. With annualized tracking error of more than 12 percent, the optimal portfolio would undoubtedly behave very differently from the market portfolio.

Some institutional investors, even if they have the operational capabilities, might prefer not to adopt such a portfolio. A fund manager could be worried about career risk; if he experiences a string of unfavorable returns compared to his benchmark, it may be the end of his career, regardless of whether he truly held a portfolio that can deliver a 1.5 Sharpe ratio in the long term.

The last column of table 6.2 shows the performance of an optimal Sharpe ratio portfolio, constraining the tracking error to be no more than 5 percent annually. Hence we examine what happens if we impose a limit to the deviations against our benchmark index. Our Sharpe ratio is 0.66 versus 0.48 for the benchmark. To put this 0.18 increase in perspective, it means that at equal volatility we would gain 2.68 percent (0.18 × 14.89 percent) annualized return by shifting from the benchmark to the optimized portfolio.

Building on what we have just seen, the next section will examine portfolio solutions offered in the market that exploit the benefit of factor investing but invest solely in long positions and without the use of leverage.

A Closer Look at Alternative Indices and Smart Beta Products

In the asset management industry, considerable effort is put on marketing new funds, products, and portfolio solutions. This is not necessarily a bad thing. If you find a new portfolio management technique that actually results in sustainable performance (net of fees), you offer something valuable to investors. We examine in this section the relative merits of alternative indices and so-called smart beta products (or alternative beta, exotic beta, or whatever marketing term is in vogue at the moment). We consider in all cases the longest history of returns available.

The Fundamental Index

The first example of these investment solutions has been introduced by Rob Arnott and popularized by his firm Research Affiliates. Arnott, with his colleagues Jason Hsu and John West, calls this solution the Fundamental Index and explains more about it in *The Fundamental Index: A Better Way to Invest*. Instead of using market capitalization to weigh securities, their portfolio is built by using a moving average of several non-price-based variables: dividends, sales, revenues, and book value.

The objective is to obtain a diversification of mispricing risk. Let's say you believe that large stocks in the capitalization-weighted portfolio are more likely to be overpriced and stocks that have smaller allocations are more likely to be underpriced. A traditional capitalization-weighted index will consequently overweight overpriced securities and underweight underpriced securities: exactly the opposite of what you want! Assuming that market prices eventually revert to their fundamental values—meaning the mispricing of a stock is temporary—incorrect weighting can cause a performance drag.

Ideally, a stock's importance in the market should be based on its fundamental value. But we only observe their *market* values, which will differ depending on how mispriced the stock is. Therefore a stock's importance in a market is not determined by its fundamental value but by its market price. Hence its weighting will depend on how mispriced it is relative to other stocks' mispricings. For example, assuming the entire market is overvalued by 10 percent on average, if one security within the market was overvalued by 5 percent and another by 15 percent, the former would be in fact underweighted in a capitalization-weighted index while the latter would be overweighted. A stock's overweighting in market capitalization index relative to its true but unknown fundamental weight is highly correlated to its mispricing relative to other mispricings.

It's now time to face the elephant in the room: we cannot know the true fundamental values of each security. An extreme solution would be to use an equal allocation for each stock, which would naturally break the link between allocation and mispricing. But in most cases, an equal weight portfolio is not satisfactory, as it may lead to unacceptable sector allocations or positions in small and illiquid stocks.

Research Affiliates's solution is to use other metrics (dividends, sales, revenues, and book value) that are related to a company's economic footprint but *not* determined in a stock market. We stress this last part because these variables are determined in other markets. For example, sales and revenues are driven by a company's ability to sell its product in the consumer market and book value depends on the acquisition costs of its inputs, all of which can be impacted by people overpaying and bidding up prices. Regardless, the ingenuity of the RAFI portfolio is that it gives an allocation to a company based on its economic size and is therefore more intuitive and acceptable than an equally weighted portfolio.

TABLE 6.3 Performance analysis of alternative equity indices

	FTSE RAFI U.S. 1000 Index		S&P 500 Equal Weight Index		TOBAM U.S. Maximum Diversification Index	
Start Date	January 1962		January 1990		July 1979	
End Date	June 2015		June 2015		June 2015	
Panel A: Historical performance						
Annualized average returns (%)	12.30		12.05		13.27	
Annualized volatility (%)	15.17		16.32		15.17	
Annualized Sharpe ratio	0.50		0.56		0.57	
Annualized market Sharpe ratio	0.37		0.49		0.48	
Panel B: Regression on market factor						
Annualized α (%)	2.14	**	1.59		2.50	
Market	0.94	**	1.02	**	0.82	**
Adjusted R²	0.91		0.89		0.70	
Panel C: Regression on market, size, value, and momentum						
Annualized α (%)	0.08		1.08		0.94	
Market	0.99	**	1.00	**	0.82	**
Size	−0.08	**	0.01		0.23	**
Value	0.35	**	0.31	**	0.29	**
Momentum	0.05	*	0.00		0.05	
Adjusted R²	0.97		0.95		0.76	
Panel D: Regression on market, size, value, momentum, and low-beta						
Annualized α (%)	−0.23		0.70		−0.51	
Market	0.99	**	1.01	**	0.82	**
Size	−0.08	**	0.01		0.20	**
Value	0.32	**	0.27	**	0.15	**
Momentum	0.03		−0.03		−0.08	
Low-beta	0.07	**	0.07	*	0.26	**
Adjusted R²	0.97		0.95		0.79	

The second column in table 6.3 contains the historical performance of the FTSE RAFI U.S. 1000 Index, which covers 1962 to 2015. Panel A reports that the portfolio generated an average annual return over more than fifty years of 12.30 percent with a volatility of 15.17 percent, which corresponds to a Sharpe ratio of 0.50. This compares favorably to the market index, which has had a Sharpe ratio of 0.37 over the same period.[14]

In panels B through D, we conduct factor analyses of the RAFI Index. We are using our return equation from chapter 2, putting RAFI's excess returns on the left side, our factor returns on the right side, and estimating RAFI's exposures to each factor using a regression analysis. Another way of looking at the results is to note that the combination of the factors on the right side weighted by their estimated exposures produces a portfolio that replicates the product on the left side. Viewed from this replicating portfolio perspective, α can be understood as the part of the returns that cannot be replicated by the factor portfolio. For example, a value of 0.5 percent means that we may replicate the RAFI's variations in returns, but we are missing the 0.5 percent constant returns to generate the same level of average returns that the product has. In contrast, a value of −0.5 percent means that the replicating factor portfolio outperforms it by an average of 0.5 percent.

We start in panel B with a simple analysis, using only the market portfolio as a factor. RAFI's market exposure of 0.94 indicates that the index is slightly less exposed to broad market movements than the market itself and that the best replicating portfolio consists of putting 94 percent in the market factor and 6 percent in the risk-free rate. More interesting is the estimated annualized alpha of 2.14 percent. The two stars indicate that this estimate is strongly statistically significant. So when compared only to the market portfolio, RAFI seems to generate a significant amount of value added.

Panel C reports the analysis results of RAFI Index versus the market, size, value, and momentum factors. Panel D then augments the set of factors with the low-beta strategy. In both cases, the RAFI Index is strongly exposed to the market portfolio and the value factor. It is also exposed to the low-beta factor. The negative exposure to the size factor should not cast any shadows on RAFI's performance; recall that the size factor is built using all U.S. stocks whereas the RAFI U.S. 1000 uses only the largest one thousand U.S. securities. It is therefore tilted by construction to large-capitalization stocks, resulting in the negative exposure to the small-minus-big factor.

But most important is the small and insignificant α estimates (0.08 percent and −0.23 percent). We can therefore understand the Fundamental Index as a bundle of the market portfolio, the value, and the low-beta factors. The Fundamental Index concept has been criticized as being just a value tilt in disguise, and the factor analysis seems to confirm this point. RAFI's argument stands on the premise that the economic variables used are better measures of the importance of a company than market prices. AQR co-founder Cliff Asness demonstrated that weighting by book value, for instance, is equivalent to tilting market capitalization weights using a company's book-to-market ratio relative to the aggregate book-to-market ratio.[15] He noted, "It's a neat way to explain value to a layman."

To be fair, we cheat a little when interpreting the factor analysis results. We assume we could have known in 1962 that the market portfolio plus an exposure to the value and low-beta factors would give good results over the next fifty years. But the diversification of mispricing risk underlying the Fundamental Indexing approach was not a known concept either in 1962. On the other hand, we are not claiming that RAFI has no value; the point here is not that the Fundamental Index is of no use. On the contrary: it has delivered overperformance with respect to the market portfolio over a long period of time, has a low turnover, is sold at a low fee, and its construction is transparent to investors. Rather, the point is to show that it is a bundle of well-known and thoroughly studied factors and does not deliver added performance beyond its exposure to these factors. It should be understood as a smart, cost-effective packaging of factors, not as a new finance paradigm. Also, as the portfolio simulation that will be completed in a later section shows, we can achieve more balanced factor exposures.

The S&P 500 Equal Weight Index

As stated in the previous section, an equally weighted portfolio is one way to remove the potential bias toward overpriced securities in a market capitalization–weighted index. But there are other reasons why one could be interested in an equally weighted product. In a 2009 paper in the *Review of Financial Studies*, Victor DeMiguel, Lorenzo Garlappi, and Raman Uppal show that using a mean-variance optimal portfolio, as promoted by modern portfolio theory, fails to beat a simple equally weighted portfolio in several investment universes. This noteworthy paper organizes the agenda of future research; in many ways it is similar to the paper discussed in chapter 4 that showed that most predictors could not better forecast stock market returns than a sample average. Since the paper's publication, other researchers have shown that optimal portfolios do perform better when, for instance, estimation risk is diversified by combining an optimal portfolio with the minimum variance portfolio and the equally weighted portfolio.[16] In fact, the equally weighted portfolio can be seen as an extreme case of statistical robustness: we assume there is so much statistical noise that we implicitly set all expected returns, volatilities, and correlations respectively to the same value.

Let's consider the historical performance of the S&P 500 Equal Weight Index. Over the period from 1990 to mid-2015, as reported in the third column of table 6.3, the equally weighted index had delivered an average annual return of 12.05 percent with a Sharpe ratio of 0.56, beating its market-capitalization index of all U.S. stocks with a Sharpe ratio of 0.49 for the same period. As shown by the regression results in panels B through D, the equally weighted index has a significant exposure to the market, value, and low-beta factors. In all cases, however, it fails to generate significant value added. Note that the factor exposures cannot be compared across products as they have different return histories.

The Maximum Diversification Portfolio

The firm TOBAM (Thinking Outside the Box Asset Management) uses an intuitive concept of maximum diversification, as epitomized in a 2008 paper in the *Journal of Portfolio Management*[17] by Yves Choueifaty and Yves Coignard. By definition, the optimal Sharpe ratio portfolio considers both expected returns and portfolio volatility risk. Unfortunately, more often than not, these portfolios perform poorly in practice. Much of the blame falls on the difficulty in forecasting expected returns. The TOBAM portfolio instead focuses on the *diversification of unpriced risk* source of performance. It maximizes the ratio of the weighted average volatility divided by portfolio volatility. For example, if you combine assets that all have a volatility of 20 percent and you achieve a portfolio volatility of 10 percent because low cross-correlations lead to diversification benefits, the ratio is 2. If you only achieve a portfolio volatility of 20 percent (which happens if all assets are perfectly correlated), your ratio is 1. The first portfolio offers better diversification than the second.

From 1979 to 2015, the maximum diversification portfolio generated an average return of 13.27 percent and volatility of 15.17 percent per year. Its Sharpe ratio of 0.57 compares favorably to the market portfolio's ratio of 0.48 for the same period. The portfolio delivers strongly significant exposures to the market, size, value, and low-beta factors. Even though its α is not significant in all regressions, it offers a well-balanced set of risk factor exposure, albeit without momentum.

Thinking about the maximum diversification portfolio brings us back to the need to have consistent preference and portfolio evaluation metrics. If the maximum diversification portfolio generates a higher Sharpe ratio than the optimal Sharpe ratio portfolio, it is because its construction relies on better implicit forecasts of expected returns, volatilities, and/or correlations and on better *use* of these forecasts. The maximum diversification portfolio is equivalent to the maximum Sharpe ratio portfolio if we assume that asset expected excess returns are proportional to their volatilities.[18] Therefore for a given set of expected return, volatility, and correlation forecasts, the maximum diversification portfolio will lead to a better Sharpe ratio, if imposing this restriction leads to more robust forecasts of expected returns.

Current empirical evidence on whether expected excess stock returns are proportional to their volatility remains elusive. It is possible that this relation is too small to discern, but we cannot conclude for the moment that this is a better restriction to use than others. For example, the minimum variance portfolio assumes that all expected excess returns are equal across assets. Whether the maximum diversification portfolio is a better alternative portfolio solution than the minimum variance portfolio depends on which expected return restriction is better. We do not yet have a definitive answer to this question. Nonetheless, the maximum diversification portfolio does deliver an interesting balance of risk factor exposure.

A Full Portfolio

We now consider a portfolio with multiple asset classes. We limit ourselves to publicly traded asset classes: U.S. and international equities, government bonds, commodities, and currencies.

We use the market, size, value, momentum, and low-beta factors for three different regions of developed country equity markets: Europe, North America, and the Pacific.[19] We look again to Fama and French, who recently demonstrated[20] the importance of the size, value, and momentum factors in international developed equity markets. Table 6.4 reports Sharpe ratios ranging from 0.13 to 0.89 for the value factors. The Sharpe ratios for the size factors in North America and the Pacific regions are 0.16 and 0.13, respectively, while size has been detrimental to investors' wealth in Europe with a negative ratio of −0.22. Note that the performances reported for North America are different from the ones in table 6.1. First, we consider Canada as well as the United States. Second and most importantly, the period studied is different. This is a subtle reminder of the lesson from figure 6.1: risk factors are not always profitable. However, momentum and equity low-beta factors are profitable across all regions with Sharpe ratios ranging from 0.35 to 0.86.

Consider risk factors in the government debt market. We look only at U.S. Treasury bonds in this example, but this analysis could be extended to include other sovereigns and corporate bonds. We use Treasury bonds with maturities from one year to thirty years to build two risk factors: a market capitalization–weighted market portfolio of all bonds and a term risk factor constructed by buying a ten-year bond and short selling a one-year bond.[21] The second factor captures the slope of the term structure of interest rate. We consider it a risk factor because it has been shown to be a reliable predictor of the state of the economy.[22] Both government factors generated appealing Sharpe ratios over the period from 1989 to 2015 (0.77 and 0.44, respectively).

We use momentum and carry factors in the commodity and currency markets. Commodity returns are obtained by investing in twenty-four liquid futures contracts that are the closest to maturity.[23] Currency returns are obtained by trading spot exchange rates and one-month forward contracts for sixteen developed countries.[24] To construct these factors, we use the rank-based approach. First, we rank each month's commodities *or* currencies based on the previous year's return. The weight of a commodity (currency) in its momentum factor is its rank minus the median rank, which is then scaled such that the portfolio is one dollar long and one dollar short. Momentum in the commodity market has been profitable between 1989 and 2015, with a Sharpe ratio of 0.50, whereas currency momentum has been much less interesting.

Finally, we consider factors similar to the term factor in the bond market; the basis factor for commodities and the carry factor for currencies. Basis is defined as the negative of the slope of the term structure of futures contracts.[25] The carry factor in currencies consists of buying currencies of countries with high interest rates and shorting currencies of countries with low interest rates.[26] These term structure factors have been shown to be profitable in the commodity market[27] and the currency market.[28] Indeed, their respective Sharpe ratios are 0.50 and 0.61, respectively.

We form minimum variance portfolios just as we did for our previous portfolio composed of U.S. equity factors. Looking at table 6.5, we compare its performance to the global equity market (the market capitalization portfolio of all developed country equity markets). In this case, the Sharpe ratio almost quintuples, going from 0.32 to 1.52. The leveraged portfolio, which allows factor weights to sum to 200 percent, results in an average annual return of 11.05 percent with a volatility of 7.07 percent (see note 13).

The dynamic allocations reported in figure 6.3 show that the portfolio is again close to an equally weighted portfolio of all factors (as they become available through time). Why is this simplistic portfolio so profitable? Of course, one should again be

TABLE 6.4 Historical performance of risk factors in multiple asset classes (1989–2015)

	Equity market			Equity size			Equity value		
	Europe	North America	Pacific	Europe	North America	Pacific	Europe	North America	Pacific
Historical performance of equity factors, 1989–2015									
Annualized average excess returns (%)	6.07	7.72	1.02	–1.63	1.48	1.13	2.67	1.68	9.28
Annualized volatility (%)	17.49	15.11	20.11	7.37	9.23	9.00	10.74	12.57	10.38
Annualized Sharpe ratio	0.35	0.51	0.05	–0.22	0.16	0.13	0.25	0.13	0.89
Skewness	–0.60	–0.76	0.13	–0.05	0.81	0.31	–0.12	0.83	0.19
Average correlation with other factors	0.05	0.01	0.06	0.03	0.00	0.06	–0.01	–0.02	0.00

	Equity momentum			Equity low-beta		
	Europe	North America	Pacific	Europe	North America	Pacific
Annualized average excess returns (%)	11.42	8.85	4.89	10.28	10.26	8.61
Annualized volatility (%)	13.85	16.18	14.14	11.97	12.75	11.97
Annualized Sharpe ratio	0.82	0.55	0.35	0.86	0.81	0.72
Skewness	–1.37	–1.94	–0.96	–0.12	–0.52	0.21
Average correlation with other factors	–0.01	0.01	–0.04	0.10	0.08	0.04

(Continued)

TABLE 6.4 (*Continued*)

Historical performance of bond, commodity, and currency factors, 1989–2015

	Government bond		Commodity		Currency	
	Market	TERM	Momentum	Basis	Momentum	Carry
Annualized average excess returns (%)	2.39	3.09	10.26	10.25	0.55	3.86
Annualized volatility (%)	3.11	7.03	20.57	20.67	7.32	6.38
Annualized Sharpe ratio	0.77	0.44	0.50	0.50	0.08	0.61
Skewness	-0.15	-0.07	0.14	0.51	0.10	-0.57
Average correlation with other factors	0.05	0.05	0.07	0.04	0.00	0.04

TABLE 6.5 Performance of multi-asset class optimal portfolios of factors (1989–2015)

	Global Equity Market Index	Optimal portfolio without leverage	Optimal portfolio with leverage
Historical performance, 1989–2015			
Annualized average excess returns (%)	4.93	5.54	11.05
Annualized volatility (%)	15.38	3.65	7.07
Annualized Sharpe ratio	0.32	1.52	1.56
Skewness	–0.66	–0.42	–0.42

cautious when interpreting results from historical simulations. But here we used only liquid stocks in developed markets, U.S. government bonds, and liquid commodity and currency futures. Hence this portfolio is implementable by an institutional investor and its efficiency would not be significantly hampered by a need for portfolio sampling (in order to limit the number of positions) if it were needed.

The answer lies in the diversification potential obtained by investing across risk factors and across asset classes. We often hear that diversification does not work; it's argued that diversifying by investing in different asset classes fails because these asset classes jointly generate poor performance during crisis periods exactly when their diversification properties are most needed.

But this reasoning is flawed. Asset pricing models tell us that we should diversify across priced risk factors, not across asset classes. Diversification across risk factors does work.[29] Table 6.4 reports that the average correlation of each factor with all other factors is close to zero in all cases. Figure 6.4 reports the three-year realized geometric return of the optimal portfolio

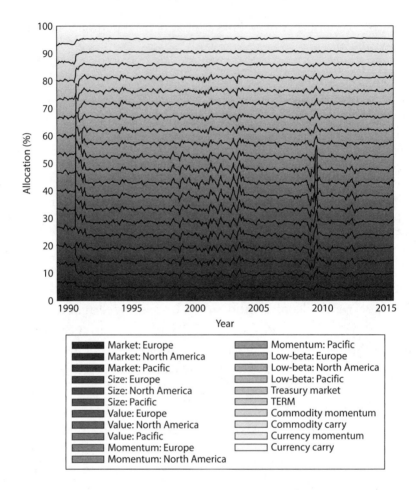

FIGURE 6.3 Allocation to risk factors in a Sharpe optimal multi-asset class portfolio

without leverage and the global equity benchmark portfolio. Consider in particular the financial crisis of 2008. Though performance suffers, the optimal portfolio offers less volatile performances and remains in positive territory. Factor diversification really works.

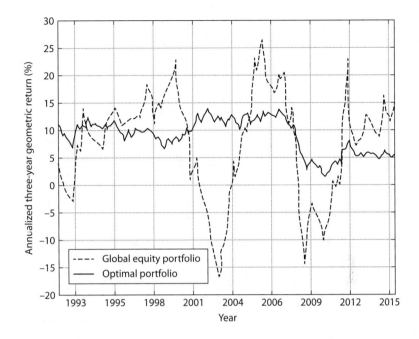

FIGURE 6.4 Three-year annualized geometric return (1989–2015)

Portfolios for a Constrained Investor

Outperformance is relative. For instance, it is easy to say that a fund manager's or product's performance can be explained by momentum. But for many retail investors and smaller institutions, momentum is hard to integrate into a portfolio. It involves frequently trading a large number of stocks or applying sophisticated sampling techniques to limit the number of stocks traded.

In these cases, a fund (mutual fund, hedge fund, or exchange-traded fund) that provides an exposure to factors may be attractive to some investors even if it has a negative α. This is not controversial. If you are a retail investor who faces high transaction costs and you try to implement a momentum strategy, you will obtain its performance minus the cost that you incur, say 1.0 percent (which includes not just transaction costs, but also other costs such as the fact that you are not working on something else while you are trading). In this instance, a fund that gives you its performance but charges management fees of 0.50 percent is a pretty sweet deal.

With that in mind, we'll now examine the performance of more constrained portfolios and consider the ability to obtain factor exposures through the exposures to traditional indices. We select indices that have liquid exchange-traded funds available. We use indices in historical simulations assuming that before these exchange traded funds were available the same exposure could have been obtained by investing in index funds.

We use indices to capture the market, size, and value factors in equity markets for three different regions: the United States, EAFE (Europe, Australasia, and the Far East), and emerging markets. We focus on market, size, and value because they've been around for a long time. There are indices that offer either an exposure to a market capitalization–weighted index or portfolio tilts related to size and value and funds that track them. We thus take into account whether an investor would have been able to invest in these indices at each point in time during our historical simulation (even now, relatively few ETFs offer pure exposure to momentum in the U.S. market, let alone in international markets).

We use a broad U.S. Treasury market index to get exposure to the government bond market factor and a U.S. long-term Treasury Index to obtain the tilt implied by the term slope factor. In commodities, we use only the S&P Goldman Sachs Commodity Index. The momentum and basis factors in the commodity market, as well as the carry trade factor in the currency market, are now available through ETFs, but given the short time series, we leave them aside.

Table 6.6 presents the starting date of each index (which varies across the indices), the ticker of one ETF that tracks this index as well as its current management fee, and the summary statistics of historical performance. The ETF management fees vary from as low as 0.10 percent per year (U.S. long-term Treasury Index) to as high as 0.75 percent (the commodity index). In the following sections, we present performances without incorporating management fees. This is because we want our results to be comparable to the ones in the previous sections for which we did not incorporate transaction and management costs. We also want our results to be indicative of potential performance, regardless of how these indices are traded. Our results can serve as benchmarks for retail investors who might buy these ETFs *and* institutions that might be able to invest in these indices at lower costs.

All Sharpe ratios are economically sizable, and all equity indices present negative historical skewness, whereas bond indices exhibit positive skewness. We now turn to long-only unlevered optimal allocations.

Until now, we have set all expected returns as equal, which is equivalent to using the minimum variance portfolio. We use this example to introduce one more layer of sophistication: using expected return predictions to find our optimal Sharpe ratio allocation. As in chapter 5, we set expected excess returns to the yield (computed over the last twelve months) without any further adjustment, which is a simplified version of a predictive model put forward by Miguel Ferreira and Pedro Santa-Clara from the Universidade Nova de Lisboa.[30] But even if this model looks oversimplified, it has had positive realized predictive power for all assets, considered over their respective histories.[31]

On one hand, we now face a common problem that plagues portfolio management: expected returns are notoriously hard to predict and portfolio weights are highly sensitive to their value. Small changes in these inputs can change allocation dramatically, and estimation errors make uncontrolled allocation perform poorly in real life. On the other hand, even if we have a perfect prediction model—meaning that we forecast expected returns, volatilities,

TABLE 6.6 Historical performance of indices in multiple asset classes

Historical performance of indices

	U.S. equity market			Canadian equity market			Europe, Asia, and Far East equity market		
	Market	Size	Value	Market	Size	Value	Market	Size	Value
Index name	Russell 1000 Index	Russell 2000 Index	Russell 1000 Value Index	MSCI Canada Index	MSCI Canada Small Cap Index	MSCI Canada Value Index	MSCI EAFE	MSCI EAFE Small Cap Index	MSCI EAFE Value Index
ETF Ticker	IWB	IWM	IWD	EWC	EWCS	XCV	EFA	SCZ	EFV
ETF management fee	0.15%	0.20%	0.20%	0.48%	0.59%	0.50%	0.33%	0.40%	0.40%
Start date	January 1979	January 1979	January 1979	January 1970	January 2001	January 1975	January 1970	January 2001	January 1975
Annualized average excess returns (%)	7.34	8.04	7.60	5.82	10.01	7.04	5.49	8.74	7.89
Annualized volatility (%)	15.24	19.54	14.64	19.73	23.97	18.94	17.02	18.76	17.37
Annualized Sharpe ratio	0.48	0.41	0.52	0.29	0.42	0.37	0.32	0.47	0.45
Skewness	-0.70	-0.81	-0.73	-0.47	-0.85	-0.31	-0.32	-0.81	-0.29

	Emerging market equity market			Government bond market		Commodity market
	Market	Size	Value	Market	Long term	Market
Index name	MSCI Emerging Markets Index	MSCI Emerging Markets Small Cap Index	MSCI Emerging Markets Value Index	Barclays U.S. Treasury Index	Barclays U.S. Long Treasury Index	S&P GSCI Commodity Index
ETF Ticker	EEM	EEMS	EVAL	GOVT	TLO	GSG
ETF management fee	0.68%	0.67%	0.49%	0.15%	0.10%	0.75%
Start date	January 1988	June 1994	June 1994	January 1973	January 1973	January 1970
Annualized average excess returns (%)	9.89	5.15	5.82	2.03	3.42	4.37
Annualized volatility (%)	23.24	23.42	23.18	5.26	10.51	19.94
Annualized Sharpe ratio	0.43	0.22	0.25	0.39	0.32	0.22
Skewness	-0.62	-0.47	-0.57	0.48	0.39	0.03

and correlations with no estimation and model error—we may still be uncomfortable with the suggested allocation that maximizes the Sharpe ratio. Would you be comfortable with a 100 percent allocation to bonds? How about a 100 percent allocation to stocks? Of course, this is a consequence of choosing the Sharpe ratio as a preference metric, which does not accommodate our degree of comfort with the magnitudes of the individual allocations.

In reality, we generally impose constraints on portfolio weights. We can therefore define our preference as maximizing the Sharpe ratio with an allocation we are comfortable with. What kind of portfolio constraints should we impose? It turns out that there is a strong relation between the kinds of constraints that investors would like to impose to be comfortable with a portfolio allocation and the kinds of constraints that lead to more robust portfolio performance from a purely statistical point of view (i.e., the ones that reduce the impact of estimation errors).

Let's consider a few examples. Few of us have the ability or the willingness to keep short positions in our personal portfolio. As it happens, imposing positive weights as a constraint when obtaining our optimal portfolio is equivalent to controlling for estimation errors in the covariance matrix of returns, which leads to more robust realized performances.[32] Alternatively, we could impose a limit on the concentration in our portfolio, measuring the concentration as the sum of squared portfolio weights. For example, the equally weighted portfolio has the lowest amount of concentration ($1/N$ where N is the number of assets in the portfolio) and a portfolio fully invested in one asset has a concentration of 1 or 100 percent. In one of their many insightful contributions to the portfolio management literature, Victor DeMiguel, Lorenzo Garlappi, Francisco Nogales, and Raman Uppal show that imposing such a constraint is equivalent to shrinking the covariance matrix, which reduces the most extreme covariance estimates.[33] Shrinking covariance matrices toward a target matrix was popularized by Olivier Ledoit and Michael Wolf,[34] who now offer their services on covariance matrix estimation through their firm Studdridge International.

What kind of limit should we use? Even if the parameter can be calibrated according to different objectives, we instead use a simple and intuitive way to impose a global constraint. As stated previously, the concentration of an equally weighted portfolio is $1/N$. Therefore we can impose that our portfolio is at least as diversified as an equally weighted portfolio of, say, five assets by constraining its concentration to be lower than $1/5$.

We could instead impose lower and upper allocation limits to each of the assets, for example, o percent to 40 percent for the U.S. equity market, o percent to 15 percent for the commodity index, and so on. This is subject to debate. While these individual limits can be imposed, we rely on a more holistic approach by imposing a limit on concentration of our portfolio. Next, we'll examine realized portfolio performances.

The Value of Expected Return Predictions

Table 6.7 presents the results from three different portfolios. First, we use the MSCI All Country World Index as a benchmark. Without any particular views or expertise, an investor can at least invest in the global market capitalization–weighted portfolio, which is available at a low cost. For example, the ETF *SPDR MSCI ACWI IMI* has a gross expense ratio of 0.25 percent.

Second, we present the performance of the optimal Sharpe ratio portfolio that uses average excess return to predict future average excess returns. This is the most naïve prediction you can make, which makes it a good benchmark to see the value added by expected return predictions. Every quarter, we use the average excess return of each asset up to the previous quarter as a prediction for the next quarter's expected excess return. As we progress through time, we have more and more returns from which we can estimate average returns of each asset. However, by taking such a long view, we omit information that may be useful about current market conditions. Finally, we report the performance of our optimal Sharpe ratio portfolio, using yields as expected excess return predictions.

The last portfolio has realized a Sharpe ratio of 0.73 for the period of January 1985 to June 2015, which compares favorably to the 0.54 for the sample-average-based portfolio and the 0.39 for the MSCI ACWI benchmark. At equal levels of volatility, the value of using our simple expected return prediction technique is 2.28 percent per year ((0.73 – 0.54) × 12.01 percent), which is substantial.

Perhaps surprisingly, the value added is reflected in lower realized volatility (8.48 percent versus 12.01 percent), not higher average excess return (6.22 percent versus 6.49 percent). Empirically, an asset with a low payout ratio (low cash payout or high price) tends to experience lower returns going forward, and an asset that falls usually experiences an increase in volatility. An allocation based on the current payout yield would advantageously allocate less to this asset than a model based only on the current level of volatility. After the asset has fallen, it will have a high payout ratio (high cash payout compared to low prices) and high volatility. Hence an allocation using this information will advantageously allocate more to this asset than an allocation based solely

TABLE 6.7 Performance of multi-asset class optimal portfolios of indices (1985–2015)

	MSCI All Country World Index	Optimal portfolio based on sample average excess return	Optimal portfolio based on payout yield
Historical performance, 1985–2015			
Annualized average excess returns (%)	5.98	6.49	6.22
Annualized volatility (%)	15.42	12.01	8.48
Annualized Sharpe ratio	0.39	0.54	0.73
Skewness	–0.72	–0.99	–0.77

on the current high volatility level. This issue is also addressed by having a risk model that incorporates mean reversion, a topic we will discuss in the next section.

Globally, these effects lead to more stable portfolio allocations than a model based only on risk measures or relying only on historical average returns. Figure 6.5 presents dynamic portfolio allocations across time, which vary depending on which assets are available at each point in time and their relative volatility and correlations, as well as their payout ratio.

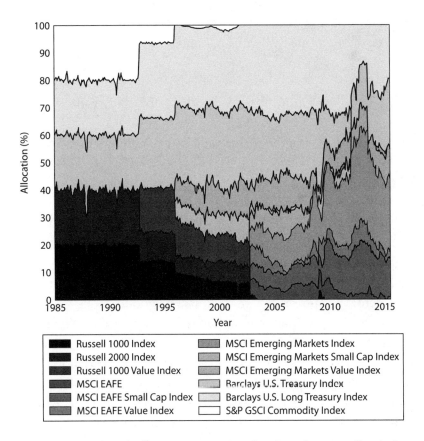

FIGURE 6.5 Optimal allocation to equity, bond, and commodity indices (1985–2015)

Is this really a good deal for a retail investor? Absolutely. The ETF fees paid, weighted by the average allocation, are 0.13 percent per year, compared to the 0.25 percent expense ratio on the MSCI ACWI ETF. This means that the increase in performance remains even when taking the ETF management fee into account. This conclusion remains even when considering another ETF as a benchmark. For example, the Vanguard Total Stock Market ETF, which tracks all U.S. stocks exactly as our U.S. market factor at the beginning of this chapter, charges 0.05 percent per year. This 0.08 percent return advantage does not adversely affect the sizable increase in risk-adjusted performance. Having established the value of using our expected excess return predictions, we now turn to the economic value of risk models.

The Value of Risk Model Sophistication

Do we really need a more sophisticated risk model than the simple one we have been using so far? To see why the answer is a resounding yes, let's examine the most ubiquitous patterns of risk in financial markets.

Volatilities and correlations vary greatly through time, and their variations are persistent; this means that when volatility is high it tends to stay high some time, and vice versa. Our exponentially weighted average, by putting more weight on recent returns, satisfactorily captures this fact. So far, so good.

However, a simple methodology based on an exponential weighted average fails in one regard: its volatility and correlation predictions are constant, regardless of the forecasting horizon. If the market has been particularly turbulent recently, I forecast it will remain volatile over the next day, month, quarter, or even year. In reality, volatilities and correlations mean revert, meaning that following episodes of high values, they tend to slowly come back down to average levels.

This mean reversion is important to capture. Let's say equity market volatility has been especially high recently, for instance, 40 percent on an annual basis. When deciding on your allocation to equity for the next year, the allocation based on a 40 percent volatility forecast would be too low: you would tend to keep a defensive position for too long. If you rightfully think that volatility is expected to slowly come back down to an average level of around 15 percent, your forecast for the next year might be something in the middle, say 20 percent or 30 percent, depending on the speed of mean reversion. This more precise forecast avoids keeping a defensive position for too long. The opposite is also true: if the market has recently been unusually calm, you would take a too aggressive position and could suffer as volatility increases back to its average level.

Using models that capture this mean reversion brings us to a crucial issue in portfolio management. Simply put: our expected return and risk predictions should be in line with our rebalancing frequency. It makes little sense to determine our rebalancing frequency separately from our allocation policy. Remember that all portfolio management techniques fall in the same mold: they optimize a preference metric subject to the investor's financial constraints and the statistical behavior of asset prices. The issue of a rebalancing policy concerns all three elements: it can be influenced by our preference metric (we can have a long investment horizon or we can simply be averse to high portfolio turnover), our financial constraints (such as high transaction costs, which make frequent rebalancing unprofitable), and returns' behavior (no momentum makes frequent rebalancing more profitable than if returns exhibit momentum). Therefore factors that determine the rebalancing policy should be included in the portfolio optimization problem from the start, not examined afterward. For instance, in this chapter we assume that we rebalance every quarter,[35] either because of our preference for lower turnover or due to financial constraints. Therefore we need to project volatilities and correlations' expected mean reversion over the next quarter. The conclusion is quite simple: an investor who is going to trade every day should not have the same allocation as an investor who is going to rebalance every year.

Another stylized pattern in financial markets is that risk is not captured only by volatilities and correlations. Volatility and correlation perfectly describe risk if returns follow a normal distribution, which is a function that describes how probable different returns are. Normal distributions are common in finance. Historically, they were used because they are easy to handle analytically (meaning that many formulas can be derived). Under some assumptions, the central limit theorem states that many probability distributions will converge to normal distributions as random shocks are aggregated. But overwhelming empirical evidence shows that returns are not normally distributed. This is not a failure of theory: the normal distribution is simply not as realistic as we could hope.

Financial econometricians work with more flexible distributions that capture asymmetries in returns (that is, skewness) and accommodate for the fact that extreme events happen more often than implied by a normal distribution. Most asset returns display more *downside risk* than *upside potential*, which is not entirely captured with volatility. Similarly, asset returns usually exhibit more *joint downside risk*, meaning that they plummet at the same time during a crisis period, than *joint upside potential*, which cannot be fully captured by correlations. Having a model with time-varying volatilities and correlations does not change these facts.[36]

While incorporating these asymmetries is done in advanced risk models, predicting time variations in return asymmetries remains difficult. This is not surprising from an economic point of view. Volatilities concern the magnitude of returns, whereas skewness is about the magnitude *and* the sign of returns. Just as forecasting the expected return is hard, forecasting skewness is even trickier. Competition among investors makes it hard to forecast the direction of returns, and the same argument applies to the problem of forecasting asymmetry risk. Short of predicting when assets are going to have more or less downside risk, the current compromise is to attempt to capture which type of assets tend to have more downside risk than others.

Peter Christoffersen of the University of Toronto and one of us (Langlois) compute the value added by a more realistic risk model for a fund that allocates across the U.S. equity market, size, value, and momentum factors.[37] This experiment is similar to those at the beginning of this chapter, but without the low-beta factor. The major difference is that they consider investors with different preference metrics than only the Sharpe ratio. The added value can reach up to 1.17 percent per year simply by switching from a basic risk model to one that is more realistic. In the highly competitive asset management industry, such an advantage can be significant. Of course, estimating these risk models requires more expertise, but using them does lead to higher risk-adjusted performance. This is good news for financial econometricians and risk managers!

These results are impressive because they are based on preferences that give little weight to downside risk. Hence the value added would be even higher for an investor who cares about the risk of large but rare negative returns or who has a value-at-risk constraint. Even when trying to maximize the Sharpe ratio, a more realistic risk model still has value because it leads to more precise volatility and correlation estimates.

This is only the starting point. Including more information into optimal portfolio allocations is a growing and promising stream of research. The risk models discussed so far are all return based, in the sense that the risk predictions are all derived using only past returns. State-of-the-art risk models also incorporate other variables such as valuation ratios and macroeconomic conditions.

Another promising and useful set of portfolio management techniques predicts portfolio weights instead of expected returns and risks. The standard approach is to separately determine which model and variables can best predict expected returns and risk measures. But the typical investor doesn't actually care about predicting each of these values. Rather, he cares about using information to predict the portfolio weights that are going to perform best. In a series of papers written with co-authors, Michael Brandt of the Fuqua School of Business at Duke University shows how *directly* modeling portfolio weights as a function of firm characteristics and economic variables can side step many of the estimation problems that afflict portfolio management.[38] For example, a *Journal of Finance* paper co-written with Yacine Ait-Sahalia of Princeton University[39] shows that the most important variables for an investor depend on his investment horizon. Momentum is important for a short-term investor, dividend yield is key for a long-term investor, and all investors, regardless of preferences, should pay attention to the slope of the term structure of interest rates.

Again, all of the previous results are only the starting point.

Other Concerns?

In this chapter, we've mainly focused on Sharpe ratio–maximizing investors with a quarterly investment horizon. But there are many other concerns that can affect optimal portfolio allocations.

Let's consider liquidity. Investors can rebalance every year (in which case they can invest more significantly in illiquid assets) or they can have short horizon (in which case liquidity and market structure matter a lot). We use middle-of-the-road examples in this chapter: investors who rebalance every quarter in all traded assets but the highly illiquid. We have not touched on allocation techniques for investors who invest in both liquid and illiquid assets.[40] For an excellent treatment on the role of liquidity in asset management, see Andrew Ang's *Asset Management*.[41]

Another issue in asset management is whether one should hedge currency risk. A position in an international asset can be seen as a long position in the asset denominated in its local currency and a long position in the foreign currency. Nothing fundamentally changes from what we have seen so far. The portfolio optimal allocation can be derived using all assets denominated in the investor's home currency. Outright positions in foreign currencies can be used to improve the preference metric of the portfolio, just as *any other asset* can be added to achieve such improvement.

For example, an allocation to international equities held by a Canadian investor will be different from the allocation of a U.S. investor. This difference is driven by the unique behavior of each currency. The Canadian dollar is pro-cyclical, meaning that it tends to increase when the world equity market increases and decrease when the world market falls. Hence hedging the implied currency exposure is not necessarily appealing because currency fluctuations act as a hedge for the international equity exposure of a Canadian investor. When the world market portfolio falls in value, the price of foreign assets in Canadian dollars increases (i.e., the Canadian dollar depreciates), which counteracts the fall in equity value. Hedging can increase total risk from the point of view of a Canadian investor.

In contrast, the U.S. dollar is a counter-cyclical currency. It tends to act as a safe haven by gaining in value when the world market falls. The losses on international investments are amplified for a U.S. investor because the currency in which the foreign assets are denominated fall in terms of U.S. dollars as the same time that the asset values fall. Therefore a U.S.-based investor would have a greater preference for hedging his foreign currency exposure to reduce risk.

One should realize that beyond the obvious exposure to the foreign currency in which the foreign asset is denominated, we are also exposed to other currencies through the nature of the asset (for example, a firm's sales in other countries). Precisely understanding

our foreign currency exposures is a daunting task, and it is therefore not possible to measure all currency exposures. The big decision is whether you take positions in foreign currencies in general.
If you do, the correlations with other assets in your investment
universe will determine your currency hedging needs.

To illustrate this point, consider a Canadian investor. Table 6.8
reproduces the experiment of table 6.7, in which we examined
the value added by using yield-based expected return predictions
on optimal portfolios. The difference here is that we compute the
optimal allocation using asset returns denominated in Canadian
dollars. We also make two changes to the investment universe.
First, we add the MSCI Canada Index, the MSCI Small Cap
Index, and the MSCI Value Canada Index to capture the fact that
Canadian investors may have a home bias. Second, we change
the two government bond indices to Canadian government bond
indices.[42]

The conclusion reached in the previous section remains true.
Our optimal CAD-denominated portfolio beats the one using
sample average returns and the Canadian equity market used as
a reference.

In figure 6.6, we report the portfolio betas (i.e., the risk exposures) of three different currencies,[43] computed using our optimal

TABLE 6.8 Performance of multi-asset class optimal portfolios of indices
in Canadian dollars (1987–2015)

	MSCI Canada Index	Optimal port-folio based on sample average excess return	Optimal port-folio based on payout yield
Historical Performance, 1987–2015			
Annualized average excess returns (%)	5.11	5.23	5.03
Annualized volatility (%)	15.21	10.08	7.00
Annualized Sharpe ratio	0.34	0.52	0.72
Skewness	−0.92	−0.94	−0.72

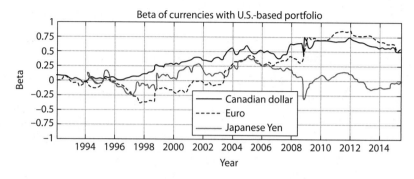

FIGURE 6.6 Beta of major currencies with U.S. and Canadian portfolios (1992–2015)

portfolio (the last column in tables 6.7 and 6.8). For the U.S.-based portfolio we use the Canadian dollar, the Euro (constructed using European currencies before its introduction), and the Japanese Yen. For the Canadian-based portfolio, the Canadian dollar is replaced with the U.S. dollar.

Currency betas are largely positive for the U.S. portfolio, which implies that these currencies should be short sold to minimize the portfolio risk. This is in line with the intuition given earlier. The portfolio holds foreign assets and is by construction exposed to foreign currencies. By shorting these currencies, we reduce (or hedge) the exposure.

These betas are in contrast with the betas found in the bottom graph for the Canadian-based portfolio in which the majority is negative. Hence to minimize the volatility of the portfolio, these currencies should be bought. We should *increase* the currency positions already taken by investing in foreign assets. This would actually be quite expensive, as all three currencies have depreciated against the Canadian dollar over this period, but it would have dampened volatility.

Inflation could be another concern. A pension fund might have payments that are indexed to inflation promised to its retirees, while an individual investor saving for retirement will care about protecting his purchasing power.

Unfortunately, inflation hedging is elusive. Correlations between inflation and our predictions for good inflation hedges are not high. Gold is a poor inflation hedge,[44] the evidence for real estate and commodities is mixed, and even inflation-protected bonds, such as Treasury Inflation-Protected Securities in the United States or Real Return Bonds in Canada, are not that effective due to their illiquidity and the volatility of the real rate of return, and they may be too expensive for their hedging ability. Short-term government bills, on the other hand, seem to be good inflation hedges, but the expected return is also quite low.

Just as we added constraints on portfolio weights, we can adjust our portfolio management approach in different ways to reflect inflation concerns. First, we can, of course, ensure that we have inflation-hedging assets in our universe of possible assets, just as we added currencies in the case of currency hedging. Next, we can integrate our inflation concern into our portfolio management technique either by adjusting our preference metric or by imposing a new constraint. The former is not obvious; we would need to combine our basic preference metric (e.g., Sharpe ratio) with the notion of inflation-adjusted returns. Alternatively, one can impose a constraint such that our portfolio should have a positive correlation with inflation, meaning that certain assets with inflation-hedging abilities will be favored in the optimal allocation. Still, incorporating inflation concerns remains a challenge.

A Note on the Use of Derivative Products in Portfolio Management

A derivative product is a financial contract whose value is derived from the value of another value, such as a stock or bond price, the weather, or the value of a commodity. The distinction between stocks, bonds, and derivatives is elusive. After all, a stock is also a contract whose value is derived from the income-producing capacity of a firm's assets (i.e., real assets); this capacity depends on the state of the economy and other variables. And so on.

In this chapter, we have focused on portfolios composed of basic assets (stocks, bonds, and futures). Nothing prevents us from using other derivatives in building portfolios. Nothing fundamentally changes either.

The point to understand is that once the *payoff* of the portfolio has been chosen by the investor, there are many ways of *engineering* this payoff. Some may involve only stocks and bonds and some may involve other derivatives.

For example, consider two institutions investing in a U.S. stock with the same objective in terms of payoff: one linked to the performance of this company. One institution may have a better knowledge of how to value and trade options, and it can use this expertise to make a better choice between buying the stock or an option on the stock. If it is right, it achieves the desired payoff at lower cost (i.e., a higher Sharpe ratio).

Now imagine you want to obtain the return on the S&P 500 Index over the next quarter, but do not want to lose more than 3 percent. You can buy a put option on the index and invest the rest of your wealth in the index. Alternatively, you can solve the dynamic portfolio management problem that will generate this payoff. This is much more complicated than the one-period Sharpe ratio–maximizing portfolio we have considered in this chapter. You need to model how the index varies each minute, hour, or day and compute the optimal position in the stock market to hold at each point in time to generate the desired payoff at the end of the quarter. If you succeed, you will find that the optimal portfolio looks like the replicating portfolio of a long position in the market plus the same put option. Indeed, valuing a put option or finding the dynamic portfolio that generates the desired protection is equivalent. In fact, there is very little difference between the techniques used in the literature on dynamic portfolio management and on option pricing. For a retail investor who may also have other preoccupations, buying a put option is certainly cheaper than creating the put option through frequent dynamic trading.

Still, considering options does not alter our discussion of portfolio management set so far in this book. Appropriately considering our three sources of sustainable performance can be achieved by incorporating options in a portfolio. Some risk factors may only be extracted by trading options, but we do not cover this topic in this book.

Concluding Remarks

At one extreme, we have examined the issue of institutional investors concerned with owning complex portfolios of long and short positions across asset classes and with the use of reasonable leverage. In doing so, we have used much of our current understanding of finance literature and evidence from decades of portfolio management experience. We also considered the situation of investors who are more constrained, more preoccupied with tracking error (i.e., looking different) and career risk. Although retail investors do not have access to the full range and efficiency of factor-based long-short portfolios, there are many reasonably priced investment products that offer appropriate factor tilts. Furthermore, they are available at levels of overall MERs as low as those of many large institutional investors.

We have shown that all categories of investors could achieve higher levels of Sharpe ratios on their portfolios. Nevertheless, it may be optimistic to believe Sharpe ratios as high as 1.5 could be reached. Such portfolios require investing across portfolios of factors using short positions and gross leverage. Many institutional investors would hesitate to implement such portfolios because of short-term business risk and internal political reasons. However, our personal experience in designing efficient portfolios illustrates that it is possible to achieve Sharpe ratios close to one on unlevered balanced products subject to allocation policy constraints that make full use of relevant factor tilts and more sophisticated risk management and predictive methodologies. There is a middle ground, but we'll explain in chapter 7 why it remains a challenge to push for products that are built on the principles we just discussed.

To a large extent, we have contributed to democratize the asset management process. Performances of active managers and of smart beta products can largely be explained by the underlying diversification processes used consciously or unconsciously by these managers and products, which lead to very specific risk factor tilts. Once we understand that a significant part of our skill requirement is to have an understanding of relevant risk factors and of methodologies to efficiently exploit and integrate these factors within a portfolio, the sources of alpha become more transparent and high fees are more difficult to justify.

7

We Know Better, But . . .

Investing is simple, but not easy.

—Warren Buffett

DARSE BILLINGS IS A Canadian computer scientist with a Ph.D. in computer poker from the University of Alberta. His research interests include abstract strategy games. His program "Mona" became the world champion of "Lines of Action" in 2000 when it defeated the best human players and won every game. Billings is credited with saying the following about poker:[1]

> There is no other game that I know of where humans are so smug, and think that they just play like wizards, and then play so badly.

Many in the investment management industry also fall into this trap of self-assurance.[2] Even worse, it is only one of the many biases that we as investors are afflicted with. This chapter examines many of our flaws, cognitive biases, heuristics we rely on, and errors we make as investors. The objective is to show that even though we understand and perhaps agree on the investment ideas we have discussed in previous chapters, we can fail in implementing them in real life, either in our personal portfolio or in large and sophisticated institutions.

Although this chapter discusses cognitive biases investors exhibit, our discussion differs from what you usually find in a behavioral finance book. We usually discuss how the bounded rationality of investors influences their trading behavior. Here we instead focus on the factors that can influence whether the investment approach discussed in this book can be adopted by institutional investors.

According to Charley Ellis, "Successful Investing does not depend on beating the market. Attempting to beat the market will distract you from the fairly simple but quite interesting task of designing a long-term program of investing that will succeed at providing the best feasible results to you."[3] The more we obsess over short-term performance and forecasting, the less likely we are to achieve our long-term objectives and even, perhaps, outperform the market. Unfortunately, economic agents like investors, managers, advisors, or any decision maker are often entrenched in their beliefs, which complicates the accumulation of a coherent and generally accepted body of knowledge.

In previous chapters, we have made the case in favor of building investment processes based on three sustainable structural qualities. If we recognize the counterproductive impact of high fees and the role of luck in achieving investment success and agree that few managers are able to consistently generate value added, we must also conclude that it is unwarranted to pay high fees for portfolio management expertise that is not truly unique and can be replicated cheaply through structured investment processes.

We may agree with all of the above and still be unable or unwilling to implement investment processes that lead to efficient and appropriate portfolio solutions. The explanations lie in our own psychological traits and thinking process, an industry that promotes business philosophies at the expense of investment philosophies, and a lack of expertise and knowledge in many decision makers that find themselves unable or unwilling to challenge the status quo. Often being wrong while following the crowd appears less risky.

Chapter 7 is divided in three sections. First, we discuss the limits of human rationality and the many cognitive biases and mental shortcuts (heuristics) we rely on. Humans are not perfect rational beings. Investors do not make consistent and independent decisions, and they are subject to biases and emotions. Second, we closely examine how the confirmation bias reveals itself in the asset management industry. The content of these two sections will lead us to the last section in which we discuss the implementation requirements of a more efficient investment process for the benefits of investors.

The Limits of Human Rationality

We often underestimate the impact of heuristics, emotions, motivations, social influence, and limited abilities to process information on the integrity of our decision-making process. For example, you may recognize yourself in one or many of the following contexts:

- We prefer not to buy recent losers: we find it emotionally easier to buy an asset that has generated recent gains than one that has generated recent losses.
- We prefer to sell recent winners: we find it emotionally easier to sell an asset that has generated a gain than to sell one that has generated a loss. We hope our losing positions will eventually be proven right.
- We attribute successes to our superior skills and our failures to bad luck or market irrationality. We advertise our successes while we hide our failures. We also spend more effort to understand why we underperformed than why we overperformed because we believe success is attributed to our superior skills, while failure is caused by bad luck.

- We evaluate the actions of others according to their personality but our own as a function of circumstances. We will more easily accept that someone selling a losing asset has panicked, while we will rationalize doing the same as managing risk or abiding by some internal constraint.
- We look for sources of information that will reinforce our prior beliefs and disregard those that challenge them. Republicans are more likely to watch Fox News than MS-NBC, while most Democrats are likely to do the opposite. Both networks appear more inclined to invite guests that agree with their views and biases.
- We believe more information leads to greater accuracy even though the evidence shows that it is self-confidence that grows with information, not accuracy. Experts have difficulty accepting that often just a few factors explain most of the variability in returns.
- We rewrite history. If our views are proven wrong, we will look for that part of our reasoning that supports the observed outcome and even adapt our prior story. We also take credit for an accurate forecast even if it was the result of faulty reasoning or plain luck. We may emphasize the fact that we had anticipated a weakening of financial conditions in 2007–2008, while ignoring that we were wrong about the amplitude of the crisis. We may have forecasted that oil prices would weaken temporarily in 2014 because of a seasonal increase in inventory, while not anticipating a decline of 50 percent.
- We anchor our estimates in initial values that may not be relevant. An interesting study looked at the sentences given by experienced criminal judges when prosecutors asked for either a twelve- or a thirty-six-month sentence on very similar cases.[4] When prosecutors asked for a longer sentence recommendation, the judge attributed a sentence that was eight months longer on average, indicating that judges

were influenced not only by the evidence, but also by the request of the prosecutor. In finance we anchor our fundamental valuations on current pricing, future trends on past trends, and strategic asset allocation and product innovations on what friends, colleagues, and competitors do.

In his book *Thinking, Fast and Slow*,[5] the Nobel Prize–winning psychologist Daniel Kahneman wrestles with flawed ideas about decision making. In the 1970s, it was broadly believed that human beings were rational, but that emotions were responsible for making them act irrationally. When the stakes are high enough, people will focus and make good decisions. Economic models mostly relied on rational decision-making agents. But Kahneman questioned whether investors make choices and decisions by maximizing the net present value of future benefits of their actions and whether they understand the potential long-term consequences of their daily actions.

Kahneman and his colleague Amos Tversky showed that people making decisions under uncertainty do not act rationally.[6] In a series of experiments they identified many cognitive biases that distort our judgment, while never going as far as saying that humans are irrational. These cognitive biases are not necessarily flaws, but perhaps evolutionary adaptations to our environment.[7]

Following a large number of empirical studies in the fields of psychology and neuroscience, there has been in recent years much improvement in understanding human thought. According to Kahneman, emotions shape the way in which we think and make decisions; emotions precede logic, not the other way around.

In his book, he describes the idea of System 1 and System 2 within the human brain. System 1 is the emotional, intuitive, and fast-thinking process that allows us to successfully navigate much of our daily life. System 2 is our controlled, slow-thinking, and analytical process. While System 1 is effortless, essentially unconscious thought, System 2 requires conscious effort; System 1 is the habitual, System 2 is a goal-directed system. These systems are abstract representations that help us understand the process of decision making; they do not necessarily correlate to specific areas of the brain.

System 1 governs most of our life. As we learn and repeatedly use new skills, they become internalized, automatic, and unconscious. System 1 provides an immediate environmental impression so that we may quickly respond to our surroundings; the system is efficient, but far from infallible.

On the other hand, System 2 is slow but able to perform more complex tasks. Kahneman uses the examples of 2 + 2 and 17 × 24 to illustrate both systems. Most individuals do not think about 2 + 2; the answer 4 comes automatically. However, computing 17 × 24 generally requires greater mental effort. The relative efficiency of System 1 and System 2 is very much a function of individual skill, training, and learning by association. A grand chess master may be able to look at a chessboard and see that you will be checkmate in two moves. However, most of us would need to expend concerted effort and thought on the problem, some unable to ever reach the chess master's conclusion. We therefore rely on System 2 to tackle this intellectual challenge, but also find evidence that System 1 can be improved over time.

Though System 2 monitors System 1, it usually only endorses the actions generated under System 1. System 2 is in principle the master of System 1, but it is also lazy. A continuous effort from System 2 is mentally and physically demanding. When driving at a low speed on an empty road, System 1 will do most of the work. However, when driving in a blizzard on snow-covered roads in bad visibility, System 2 will engage, leaving the driver mentally and physically exhausted.

When System 1 is left unchecked by System 2, errors in judgment may occur. Decisions made under System 1 lack voluntary control; this can be problematic, considering how often System 1 is employed to make decisions. Because System 1 is on automatic mode, it is also responsible for many of the biases we have and for errors in judgment we make. System 1 believes that it possesses all the necessary information. Kahneman refers to this bias as WYSIATI (What You See Is All There Is); decisions are made on the basis of sparse and unreliable information. System 1 allows personal feelings to influence our judgment of a speaker's credibility, while also allowing an individual's beliefs or occupation to influence our personal feelings about them.

Impressions from System 1 are fed to System 2. Whenever System 1 senses an abnormal situation, System 2 is mobilized to protect us. In principle, System 2 can override the inaccurate impressions of System 1, but System 2 may be unaware that System 1 is misled in its conclusions. Because System 2 is unable to always identify or correct System 1's mistakes, it is not necessarily the ultimate rational tool used by economists. For example, because the average individual is usually not good at all with probabilities and statistics, we simplify our judgments such that System 1 can handle complex situations using heuristics, that is, simple and practical but not necessarily accurate methodologies.

As an illustration, Kahneman recalls an experiment called "the Linda problem." Participants were told the imaginary Linda was a single, outspoken, bright individual who as a student was deeply concerned with the issue of discrimination and social justice. Participants were then asked if it were more likely that Linda is a bank teller or if Linda is a bank teller that is active in the feminist movement? Eighty-five percent of the students at Stanford's Graduate School flunked the problem by selecting the second answer even though we know that all bank tellers who are active in the feminist movement are by definition bank tellers. The second answer better fits our perception of Linda's personality; System 1 engaged in the story, while System 2 remained inactive, allowing us to jump to a false conclusion.

Another example is the problem of the baseball and the baseball bat. Together they cost $1.10 and the bat costs $1 more than the ball. What is the cost of the ball? Most people unthinkingly answer 10 cents, allowing System 1 to think for them. However, carefully thinking about the question statement reveals that the ball must cost $0.05 such that both together cost $1.10. Again, System 2 did not step in when it should have.

There may be a reason for the sluggishness of System 2. According to neuroscientists, the parts of the brain associated with emotion are much older than those associated with logic.[8] The evolutionary need for emotion preceded the need for logic. James Montier of GMO uses the example of the snake behind the glass: when it jumps and strikes the glass, you will react, though you aren't in any real danger. System 1 assesses the threat and tells you to step back before System 2 realizes that it is not necessary.

Below is a list of personality traits, cognitive biases, and heuristics we have observed in investors (including the two of us) during our careers. Kahneman provides in his book a more thorough discussion of heuristics and biases. Most of them also make implicit references to our imperfect understanding of probabilities and statistics. Here our discussion centers on the world of portfolio management.

- *Paying too little attention to prior probabilities*: We often misuse new evidence and inappropriately adjust probabilities we attach to different events. Some investors listen to stories from fund managers, like the great trade they did last quarter, and attach too much weight to them compared to the base probability of a fund manager being talented.
- *Paying too little attention to sample size*: Many of us rely on a track record of three to five years to determine a fund manager's talent, but as discussed in chapter 3, standard statistics indicate that it is almost impossible to infer

any conclusion from such a small sample. Yet many of us believe it is sufficient evidence of a manager's talent.

- *Illusion of correlation*: When Kahneman examined the performance of twenty-five advisors working at a wealth management firm, he could not find any correlation between their performance ranking in a specific year with their ranking any other year, indicating that no advisor displayed more skills than any of his peers. Yet bonuses were paid based on short-term performance. Though the firm's management did not expect a high correlation, they were surprised to find none at all; they had never attempted to collect such data.

- *Misconception about predictability*: We believe we can predict what is unpredictable: "This firm will be the next Google." Yet no one could have predicted that Google was the next Google, even its founders. Indeed, Larry Page and Sergey Brin were willing to sell their company for less than $1 million a year after its founding, but the buyer thought the price too high.

As discussed in chapter 4, we can predict what is the most likely event or characteristic of the distribution of likelihood of different events, but the event itself is unpredictable. During a 2013 investment innovation conference, Craig Pirrong, professor of finance and energy specialist at the University of Houston, presented his views of the energy sector and started with the following statement: "I hope I will be lucky or that you have a short memory."[9] Craig understood that even though his forecasts were grounded in his greater understanding of the energy industry, our track record at understanding what can be predicted, especially in complex systems (the new world order and the energy industry certainly qualify), is dismal and marred with distortions, an opinion shared by the trader-philosopher-statistician Nassim Taleb.

- *Misconception of regression to the mean*: We prefer assets or funds whose recent performance has been exceptionally good. We shun those whose recent performance has been exceptionally bad. If these exceptional performances are simply luck (high or low ε), it is not indicative of future performance.[10] Imagine that a manager has just been extremely lucky. His expertise lies in spotting undervalued companies, but he was uniquely positioned to profit from the plunge in oil prices, which he did not fully anticipate. Subsequently, his performance is less stellar. Has he lost his edge? Not necessarily. It is just regression to the mean at work. His previous outperformance is more likely to be followed by less impressive outperformance. It was luck and thus not indicative of future outperformance. Yet many of us would mistakenly conclude that this fund manager has necessarily lost his edge.

- *The availability heuristic*: The availability heuristic describes our tendency to attribute a higher probability to an event that can be easily recalled or understood. We tend to attribute more weight to what we are familiar with even though it may not be as relevant, and vice-versa. Many investors confuse investment philosophies and investment methodologies. An investor not familiar with quantitative processes is more likely to dismiss this approach compared to a fundamental approach even though both may be targeting the same investment style with different methodologies.

The availability heuristic also explains why it is so hard for us to recognize our limited forecasting ability. This is because we tend to remember forecasters whose predictions turned out to be right and forget those that turned out to be wrong. It is easier to recall the first instance than to recollect all of those whose predictions have failed. Hence we overestimate our average forecasting ability.

- *Inferring the general from the particular*: Many asset management firms have a large number of products on their platform. Because all products do not outperform (and perhaps few do outperform in the long run), they have the ability to market those products that have recently outperformed, maintaining a positive profile for the firm at all time. Many investors mistakenly have more favorable views of the global performance of this firm's funds.

Another example comes from the survivorship bias in performance data. Some firms maintain a database of historical funds' performances, for instance hedge funds. When a fund closes its doors due to poor performance, its performance can either be kept in the database or its entire history can be dropped. In the latter case, our assessment of the overall performance of hedge funds would be too favorable because it would overlook the ones that performed poorly.

- *Confusing personal preferences with an investment's risks and benefits*: Our own evaluation of the attractiveness of an investment may be tainted with our personal views. For example, we can view technologies that we like as lower risk investments than those that we don't. We can attribute a higher value to risky technologies that are still in their infancies. Renewable energy is generally an attractive idea, but it took a long time for profitable business models to emerge.
- *Illusion of understanding or the outcome bias*: We often revise our prior understanding of events given what has happened, forgetting what may have happened but did not.

The financial crisis of 2007–2009 is a perfect example. There is a good reason we say "crisis" and not "recession" or "downturn." By definition, a crisis requires that the causes are hard to discern and the consequences hard to predict, otherwise the events do not unfold into a crisis. Let's say that enough economists, policymakers, and financiers are able to spot the problems that subprime lending could create. They act by either publicizing their analysis, instituting new regulations, or trying to benefit from their information in financial markets (by short selling subprime lending related securities for example), all of which diminishes the causes and likelihood of a potential crisis. To turn this into a crisis requires that these actions do not happen to a large enough extent, that not enough people *knew* there would be a crisis.

Yet many people, with the benefit of hindsight, say that they knew either the crisis would happen or that it was obvious that it would happen. Knowing the causes and the fact that it happened, of course it is obvious that the crisis happened. We also like to rewrite history by turning our previous "I expect a weakening of credit conditions" into "I knew that there would be a financial crisis." We also often fail to take into account other risk buildups in the system that may cause a dramatic event that actually did not happen or has not yet happened.

- *Hostility to algorithms*: We have already touched on this issue in chapter 4. Experts dislike statistical approaches because they democratize the ability to explain and predict and hence reduce people's reliance on their opinion. In many instances, a statistical algorithm based on a small set of explanatory variables left unaltered by the subjective opinions of experts will perform better. It does not mean that investment experts are not needed; we still need to determine the nature of these simple models and the variables that should be used. Rather, it is that altering the results with subjective opinions often does not improve the results.

Simple algorithms are already pervasive in our economy. Genius in Apple iTunes is the result of a relatively simple algorithm that evaluates music taste based on the predefined characteristics of songs listened to in the past. Many financial products are now built around relatively simple methodologies (Fundamental Indexing, equal weight allocations, equal risk allocations, etc.).

- *The illusion of validity*: Complex systems, such as financial markets, are hard to understand and predict. Many managers believe they will achieve better forecasts if they compile more information. Having more information may make you feel that the conclusion you reach is more valid, but adding more variables may not necessarily increase the explanatory power of your model. In many cases, using complex models with many variables to understand complex systems illustrates an inability to identify the most relevant factors. Such an approach is likely to succumb to data mining, the idea that if we test enough variables, we will eventually find a pattern, albeit a spurious one.

This effect is well known to statisticians. Adding more variables that do not add additional information to a model may appear to boost its explanatory power unless we explicitly control for such phenomenon.

- *Our bias against the outside view*: When confronted with a complex situation, experts are more likely to extrapolate based on their unique experience (the inside view), often leading to overoptimistic forecasts. Kahneman in what he calls the planning fallacy, examines how we overestimate benefits and underestimate costs of outcomes. We tend to ignore pertinent input, actual outcomes observed in previous, similar situations (the outside view). Is it more reliable to estimate the cost of remodeling a kitchen based on the components you believe would be involved or would it better to inquire about the cost of several similar projects?

Let's consider the financial crisis. When it occurred, most were faced with a situation they had never experienced. Economic forecasters were making overly optimistic predictions on how quickly the economy would recover. However, Carmen and Vincent Reinhart looked at the behavior of economic growth, real estate, inflation, interest rates, employment, etc. over a twenty-year period in fifteen countries that lived through a financial crisis after WWII, as well as considering two global crises (1929 and 1973).[11] They used these examples as benchmarks to determine what could happen after the most recent crisis. The results were more accurate than most had initially expected.

Although the reality of these biases is confirmed by well-designed empirical tests, how do we understand and avoid them? Heuristics alone cannot explain all of the behaviors observed in our industry. The next section further discusses the role of the confirmation bias and its interaction with investment experts' incentives and conflicts of interests.

Different Forms of the Confirmation Biases

In many circumstances the biases discussed in the previous section also serve one's interests.[12] Individuals will often seek or interpret evidence in ways that are partial to their existing beliefs or expectations. This trait, known as the confirmation bias, is possibly the most problematic aspect of human reasoning. This confirmation bias can be impartial (spontaneous) or motivated (deliberate, self-serving), perhaps even unethical.

When the confirmation bias is impartial, evidence is gathered and analyzed as objectively as possible, but it is unconsciously subjected to biases. When the confirmation bias is motivated, evidence supporting a position is gathered and purposely accorded undue weight, while evidence to the contrary is ignored or minimized. According to John Mackay, "When men wish to construct or support a theory, how they torture facts into their service!"[13] Of course, confirmation bias can be either impartial *or* motivated. Cognitive biases alone cannot fully explain the existence of self-serving biases, but they may provide the means by which our own (biased) motivations have the capability to impact our reasoning.[14]

What is the source of motivated confirmation biases? "It is psychology's most important and immutable behavioral law that people are motivated to maximize their positive experiences and minimize their negative ones." Individuals remember their decisions and actions in ways that support their self-view. When they cannot appropriately promote themselves or defend their interests, they will misremember or reconstruct events and circumstances and make excuse for poor performance along the lines of: "I would have been right if not for . . ." or "I was almost right but something happened." Individuals' interests can be classified in many categories, but the most important levels of interests are those related to Global Self-Esteem, Security, Status, and Power, and finally Respect, Affluence, and Skills. Montier uses a more colorful nomenclature such as pride, envy, greed, and avarice, all of which can lead to confirmation biases.

Another source of motivated confirmation bias is peer pressure. Research has shown that when individuals are confronted with a group answer that they believe to be wrong, one-third of them will still conform to the answer of the group. Similarly, standing alone with a distinctive opinion is painful to us. Neuroscientists have found that maintaining an opinion opposed to the majority stimulates a region of the brain most closely associated with fear. Therefore it is easy to imagine why we may succumb to anchoring.

Unfortunately, all of these circumstances are present in our industry. We have witnessed cases of strong-willed individuals swaying entire groups in the wrong direction, leading in several cases to extremely costly consequences. Groups can easily succumb to anchoring and tunnel vision. The first individual in a group discussion to express a strong opinion can strongly influence decision making (intimidation), narrow the set of alternatives being considered (tunnel vision), and intimidate/attract support from less knowledgeable and less confident participants (anchoring) even if he is not the individual with the highest authority. If you act as an advisor during one of those meetings, you may attempt to present other arguments and hint at potential consequences, but you cannot necessarily challenge an officer of this firm (your client) if no one else within this firm dares challenge his views. The same process occurs if, as a manager, you notice incorrect statements were made by an overconfident advisor in front of his client. Will you challenge this advisor if it can cost you a portfolio mandate and if it is likely the client is unable to understand the nature of the conversation even if it would be in the best interest of the client?

There exists a great deal of literature supporting confirmation biases, and those who have spent enough time in the corporate world have run into some form or another. We will provide a few examples.[15] However, we always have to remain aware that some biases can be intentional, while others are the product of System 1.

Restricting Our Attention to a Favored Hypothesis

This occurs when we are strongly committed to or familiar with a particular opinion, allowing ourselves to ignore other alternatives or interpretations. Failing to examine other interpretations is the most prevalent form of confirmation bias. Let's consider a few examples.

Example 1—Chapters 5 and 6 supports the case for an integrated portfolio management process across asset class factors and for the asset allocation process itself. This implies that a properly structured balanced product of asset classes or factors is far more efficient than a piecemeal approach. However, most portfolio structures in our industry are designed around the concept of specialized asset class buckets (such as fixed income, equity, real estate, other alternatives) because of the belief that it is more efficient to manage the asset allocation process as a fully independent function. The investment policies of many organizations make it difficult, sometimes impossible, to integrate balanced products in their portfolios. Of course, the consulting industry is not fond of an integrated approach either because it removes part of their contribution to manager selection and asset allocation. It is not as profitable a business model for them. Even advisors have conflicts of interest.

Example 2—Every quarter, managers often explain their performance in front of investment committees. Presenting a favorable performance is gratifying and favorable performances generate far fewer questions by investment committee members than unfavorable performances. Have you ever heard an investment committee member saying: "This performance is very good but I worry about the level of risk that was required to achieve it. Could you explain?" or "Could your outperformance be the result of a benchmark that is not representative of your investment style?" Rarely is the benchmark itself a subject of deep discussions. However, when we compare the performance of a portfolio to a benchmark, we should always ask: "Is the portfolio outperforming the benchmark or is the benchmark underperforming the portfolio?"

Table 7.1 illustrates this aspect. It again presents the three measures of alphas for the FTSE RAFI U.S. 1000 Index shown in table 6.3. One measure of excess return is largely positive, while the two others are close to zero. One is even slightly negative. As we already indicated, there is nothing wrong about having a small α as long as the sources of returns are understood, investors have the desired exposure to the risk factors, and they do not pay excessive management fees for exposure to risk factors. The sources of performance in the RAFI products have been well

TABLE 7.1 Measures of excess return (1979–2015)

Excess return against the market factor only	Excess return using a four-factor model	Excess return using a five-factor model
+2.14%	+0.08%	−0.23%

documented and the licensing fees to institutional investors are very reasonable.

However, most managers do not disclose their factor exposure and all excess return is presented as α. Over the years, we have come to realize that not all institutions use fair or representative benchmarks. Because compensation is related to outperforming a benchmark, there is much incentive by managers to choose a reference point that is more likely to be outperformed over the long run. The following situations have been observed in several organizations:

- A fixed income portfolio with almost no Treasury securities benchmarked against an index with a large allocation to Treasuries;
- A mortgage portfolio benchmarked against a fixed income index also containing a large allocation to Treasuries;
- An equity portfolio benchmarked against a combination of cash and equity without having completed a proper factor analysis to determine what is appropriate;
- A private equity portfolio benchmarked against a cash plus index in which the plus part is fairly low;
- And long biased equity hedge funds benchmarked against a cash plus index. It seems we forget common sense when we use the words "Hedge Funds."

Investors must realize that some managers are wealthy not because of their skills but because of their benchmarks.

According Preferential Treatment to Evidence Supporting Belief

This bias occurs when we give greater weight to information that supports our beliefs, opinions, or business models than to information that runs counter to them.

Example 1—In chapter 5, we mentioned the two studies on commodities published in the same issue of the *Financial Analysis Journal* in 2006. One study concluded that commodities delivered a substantial risk premium between 1959 and 2004, while the other found that the risk premium was actually negative. Two studies with different conclusions—and unsurprisingly the one favoring a higher risk premium has been cited 50 percent more often in the literature.[16]

Example 2—We have discussed the importance of having a benchmark appropriate to the portfolio policy. However, the design of certain indices can present a more favorable view to incite potential investors to invest. For example, the Hedge Fund Research Fund Composite Index (HFRI) uses a monthly rebalanced equal weight allocation to all available hedge funds. This can contribute to better risk-adjusted return for the index due to diversification benefits. However, no investor could actually achieve the same performance because it would be impossible to implement the same allocation process. Of course, the benchmark construction methodology is disclosed to investors, but we doubt that most investors fully understand the favorable impact of the methodology on measures of past performance.

Seeing Only What One Is Looking For

Unlike the previous bias, which results from a tendency to favor specific sources of information and ignore others, here the bias occurs because we unfairly challenge the validity of information that runs counter to our beliefs and support unsubstantiated or irrelevant claims that bolster our case.

Example 1—The circumstances of the last U.S. presidential election illustrate this point fairly well. Politicians and pundits tend to criticize the accuracy of polls that do not reflect their own beliefs. According to Tetlock, it is not necessarily that these individuals are close-minded, but simply that it is easy for partisans to believe what they want to believe and for political pundits to bolster the prejudices of their audience.

Nate Silver predicted the presidential winner in all but one state as well as all thirty-five senate races in 2008. In 2012, he accurately predicted the presidential winner in all states as well as thirty-one of thirty-three senate races. Nevertheless, some of Silver's critics attempted to discredit all of his conclusions by attacking his methodology. For example, the political columnist Brandon Gaylord wrote about Silver:[17]

Silver also confuses his polling averages with an opaque weighting process (although generally he is very open about his methodology) and the inclusion of all polls no matter how insignificant—or wrong—they may be. For example, the poll that recently helped put Obama ahead in Virginia was an Old Dominion poll that showed Obama up by seven points. The only problem is that the poll was in the field for 28 days—half of which were before the first Presidential debate. Granted, Silver gave it his weakest weighting, but its inclusion in his model is baffling.

However, what Silver does is simply to consider all relevant information and attribute to each component a weighting based on its strength using variables such as the accuracy of such polls in the past, sampling size, and timeliness of information. For example, the Virginia poll in question had received a low weighting in

Silver's model. His approach is based on a rigorous application of probability theory as it is being taught in most colleges.

Example 2—For many years, the Canadian mutual fund industry suffered a reputation as having one of the highest total expense ratios (TER) in the world, following a report published in a top journal.[18] Answering criticisms in a letter to the president and CIO of the Investment Funds Institute of Canada, the authors confirmed their results, indicating that total expense ratios and total shareholder costs in the Canadian industry were higher than those in Australia, Austria, Belgium, Denmark, Finland, France, Germany, Italy, Japan, Luxembourg, the Netherlands, Norway, Spain, Sweden, Switzerland, the United Kingdom, the United States, and so-called offshore domiciled funds from Dublin, Luxembourg, and various offshore locations. Furthermore, the situation in Canada is even worse because, according to the Canadian Securities Administrators, individual investors have a limited understanding of how advisors are compensated. Fortunately, new regulations may now force greater disclosure.[19] The industry has been attacking this inconvenient report for years.

The Canadian industry requested an "independent" study to challenge this perception.[20] They narrowed their intervention to the United States only because it may be difficult to challenge the observation that Canadians pay more than investors in almost all jurisdictions. The main argument of the industry is that TER in the United States do not incorporate advisory fees while in Canada they do, and by accounting for this factor, the difference with the United States may not be as significant. It has been our experience, however, that Canadian financial products are in fact more expensive than similar products in the United States. In the end, the Canadian industry has to fight the argument that TER are higher in Canada until it can restructure itself and become more competitive, no matter what reasonable evidence would show.

Own Judgment Evaluation

This bias refers to our tendency to express a higher degree of confidence than is justified by our actual performance.

Studies have shown that specialists in a wide range of fields including attorneys, physicists, physicians, psychologists, and engineers are overconfident when making professional judgments. As we mentioned in chapter 4, although investing experts are more confident in their forecasts than laypeople, they are not necessarily more accurate. Though studies show clinical diagnosis based on case statistics to be more accurate than those derived from clinical judgments, experts still have more confidence in their own judgment.[21] One exception is professions that benefit from immediate and continuous feedback (like weather forecasters), although feedback, especially negative feedback, is not necessarily welcomed.

According to Tetlock, "One of the things I've discovered in my work on assessing the accuracy of probability judgment is that there is much more eagerness in participating in these exercises among people who are younger and lower in status in organizations than there is among people who are older and higher in status in organizations. This doesn't require great psychological insight to understand this. You have a lot more to lose if you're senior and well established and your judgment is revealed to be far less well calibrated than those of people who are far junior to you."

This discussion helps us understand why the super forecasters in the Good Judgement Project discussed in chapter 4 have had much greater success than others. Tetlock used our understanding of human psychology and evidence concerning the superiority of algorithms over human judgment to design an experiment that identifies individuals trained in probabilistic thinking and suffer less from the effects of ego. They seek continuous feedback and are unafraid to challenge their own views.

They are the closest representation of human algorithms. We recommended the use of robust investment processes in chapters 6 because most of us do not possess that which is required to become a good forecaster. Process is what protects us against our own human biases. We have to remember that the obstacles to a rational process can be overwhelming, even among scientists and specialists. For example, Newton could not accept the idea that the earth could be much older than six thousand years based on the arguments that led Archbishop Usher to place the date of creation to 4004 B.C.E. "The greatest obstacle to discovery is not ignorance—it is the illusion of knowledge" (Daniel J. Boorstin). It may be that better forecasters and better scientists are among those who have fewer illusions about their own knowledge and a smaller ego.

The Requirements of a More Rational Decision Process

How can investors implement a more rational investment process in the face of the obstacles discussed so far? In principle, while it is difficult to overcome biases, it should be easier to implement a rational process for an organization than for an individual. Decisions in most organizations are often subjected to a lengthy, complex process, while many retail investors make quick, emotional, and uninformed decisions.

A provider of low-cost investment solutions to retail clients reminded us how some of his clients will quickly move their assets to another manager if the balanced portfolio solutions he offers underperformed slightly compared to another product in their portfolio. The short-term return without concerns for risk seems to be the only consideration for some uninformed investors. Tremendous efforts at financial education are required at a younger age and much better education tools than are currently available must be designed.

This being said, organizations are certainly not immune to biases. Important decisions can be pushed through by individuals even though they may be suboptimal for the corporation. Decisions are sometimes subject to committee approval in which some members may lack necessary expertise, lowering the odds of individual accountability in the case of failure, but allowing all to claim contribution to a successful endeavor.

Investment committees with overloaded agendas may simply rush through them. For example, as a manager you may be given less than twenty to thirty minutes to explain your strategy to an investment committee in order to win an approval for a mandate that could be several hundred million dollars in size. Hence we operate in an industry in which we must often oversimplify the message to the point at which a meaningless but entertaining storyline becomes more important than understanding the investment principles.

The purpose of this last section is to provide the basis for the implementation of more rational investment processes by investors and their representatives, such as CIOs, investment committees, etc. We will use the term *Management* to refer to those parties in positions of authority of allocating capital to managers and strategies. On the other hand, managers, advisors, and consultants refer to those who manage assets, sell investment products, and provide asset management services.

Managers and Advisors Are Not Your Friends

An important principle to keep in mind is that fund managers and advisors are not your friends. Their interests are often not aligned with Management's interest. Managers are selling Management a product, and they respond to their own set of incentives and are subject to biases. Alan Greenspan said the following with respect to the subprime crisis: "Those of us who have looked at the self-interest of lending institutions to protect shareholder's equity (myself included) are in a state of shocked disbelief."[22] Well, self-interest should be expected when considering the exorbitant bonuses of some individuals in financial services. Let's consider the statement by Greg Smith, former executive at Goldman Sachs: "I don't know of any illegal behavior, but will people push the envelope and pitch lucrative and complicated products to clients even if they are not the simplest investments or the ones most directly aligned with the client's goal? Absolutely. Every day, in fact." One of the messages of agency theory, which studies the relation between principals (shareholders) and their agents (management), is that the asset owner should not be surprised that the agent's primary concern is not for the client.

Even if you like your advisors on a personal level or are intimidated by their understanding of the subject, it does not mean that they should not be challenged. According to the field of evidence-based management, decisions should be made according to four sources of information: practitioner expertise and judgment, evidence from the local context, a critical evaluation of the best research evidence, and the perspective of people affected by the decision.[23] However, corporations will often implement processes recommended by advisors who have in fact little case evidence of the efficacy of their proposals. In the field of management, a senior consultant admitted that the restructuring processes they implemented in several firms made millions in revenues during the initial phase and then millions more from the same clients who had to fix the organizational issues created by the restructuring.[24] It is perplexing that some advisors require, in recommending a product to investors, a performance track record of a few years, but no such equivalent evidence for implementing new processes or strategies that they have designed themselves. In principle, the roles of advisors are to:[25]

- Provide specialized technical and subject matter expertise;
- Validate what management wishes to do or has done;
- Present, particularly to boards, unpleasant realities;
- Serve as a catalyst, facilitator, enabler, and guide to the organization.

In most cases, advisors provide support and facilitate the decision process of Management. In this process, advisors must challenge Management while Management challenges advisors, but often advisors are not sufficiently challenged. Here are two examples.

During a recent investment conference, one presentation was given on how investors should allocate their assets between tax-free retirement accounts and taxable accounts. The presenter provided the traditional advice that fixed income securities should first be allocated to the tax-free account because tax rates on interest income are usually greater than on domestic dividends and capital gains.

As recently as February 2015, when the most prevalent bond index in Canada was trading at about a 1.75 percent yield before fees, investors were still being advised the following by a national publication:

> If you have enough money to build both a registered (tax-free) and non-registered (taxable) portfolio, then investments such as bonds, GICs and high-interest savings accounts are best kept inside of an RRSP (tax-free account equivalent to an IRA), because their interest income is taxed at a higher rate. Capital gains and dividends are taxed at a lower rate, so stocks can go outside your RRSP.[26]

This may have been the appropriate recommendation when interest rates were much higher, but in mid-2015 we operated in an environment in which yields on bonds were as low as 2 percent, dividend yields on some equity products were sometimes even higher than bond yields, and equities still had an expectation of long-term capital gains while the argument was more difficult to make for bonds. Do you prefer to avoid taxes on a bond product having a 2 percent expected return that would normally be taxed at a higher rate and be taxed at a lower rate on an equity product having a 6 percent expected return? Or do you prefer to avoid taxes on that 6 percent of expected return and be taxed at a higher rate on less than 2 percent of expected return? From a return compounding point of view, it is preferable to avoid taxes on the asset that has the higher nominal expected return.

Furthermore, foreign equity usually does not benefit from a preferential tax treatment on dividends and some specialized equity products target dividend yields that could even be higher than bond yields. Hence in a low-return environment, the argument to allocate dividends paying foreign securities to the tax-free account first is even stronger, especially in the context of exchange traded funds that charge relatively similar fees on fixed income and equity products (although there must be considerations for how withholding taxes are impacting performance in different investment vehicles). Finally, if bond portfolios are more likely to produce long-term capital losses, these capital losses would be very useful within a taxable account. The point is that this traditional advice may be valid on average, but not necessarily in the current market conditions.

The second example refers to an institutional investor that asked its advisor how they could increase the risk of their portfolio. The portfolio was mostly allocated to large market capitalization global equity and investment grade fixed income. Because the portfolio already had a relatively low allocation to fixed income, the advisor initially recommended that the portfolio be leveraged using equity futures contracts in order to maintain appropriate portfolio liquidity from the fixed income component. This advice is based on the traditional assumption that fixed income securities are more liquid than equity. But the recent decade of financial research has shown how securities are subject to liquidity risk, which is the possibility that their level of liquidity may vary through time, and especially vanish in crisis time.[27] The liquidity of bonds from provincial government in Canada was minimal during the worst of the financial crisis in the fall of 2008. If liquidity was required at that moment, it was easier to trade large market capitalization stocks than these bonds. The advice provided was unfortunately based on outdated knowledge.

Traditional advice should always be challenged. These two examples are not alone either. In finance, we encounter many dubious claims, for example:

- Managers with high *active shares* have more expertise;
- A 50 percent currency hedging on foreign exposure is a neutral position;
- Managers are more likely to outperform in an environment in which there are greater discrepancies in sector returns. The statement here refers to the probability of outperforming not to the scale of outperformance;
- Quantitative management is not as effective as, or is different from, fundamental management;
- Published funds' ratings are always useful to identity future performers;
- Commodities (in general), gold, and real estate are good inflation hedges;
- The average forecasting expert brings benefit to the al location process;
- Nominal corporate profits will lag in a rising inflation environment.

Each of these statements has been challenged with existing literature. Let's consider the first four. We already mentioned in chapter 2 the study by AQR indicating that managers with a high *active share* may have a small-capitalization bias, which may explain some of the results. Furthermore, even if we ignore this aspect, performances could be explained by the fact that such funds would be more efficient at diversifying mispricing because the allocation processes of benchmark agnostic managers are generally insensitive to the impact of market prices on weights. We also discussed in chapter 6 how the pro- or counter-cyclical nature of a currency impacts the optimal currency hedge ratio of a portfolio. Hence a 50 percent hedge ratio is not necessarily a neutral position. Although active managers often say that greater volatility among sectors, countries, or securities is preferable to outperform, there is no evidence that greater volatility increases the probability of outperforming (although it will impact the scale of outperformance) by specific managers. Finally, there is no study that indicates that traditional value managers outperform systematic value investment processes. Again, the exposure to the value factor is a more significant determinant of long-term performance than the specific methodology used to achieve it.

The previous two examples are also good examples of the System 1 and System 2 discussion at the beginning of this chapter. When we no longer challenge traditional beliefs, answers are simply stimulated by System 1. Montier also mentions how expert advice attenuates the activity in areas of the brain that correlate with valuation and probability weighting. Thus, when Management is provided with advice from what is believed to be a reliable source, their System 2 is prone to get lazier. Therefore using advisors does not mitigate the responsibility of Management to remain diligent and Management should not be intimidated by the clout of advisory firms.

Managing Overclaiming and Disappointments

The human tendency to exaggerate success provides biased information, complicating Management's decision process. We sometimes overrate our ability to spot deception and distinguish the relevant from the irrelevant. As discussed in chapter 4, individuals draw attention to correct forecasts while downplaying bad predictions. Additionally, there are ways of presenting numbers in a more favorable light. We mentioned in chapter 2 that some variable annuity products guarantee a minimum return of 5 percent per year during the accumulation phase, which can be ten years or more. However, in the United States the return is compounded, while in Canada it seldom is. Canadians looking at these products may be unaware of the nuance. Yet it means the U.S. minimum guarantee over ten years is greater by nearly 13 percent of the initial contract notional (62.89 percent versus 50 percent). There are many more nuances that only emerge through a careful analysis of these contracts.

The incentive to overclaim is substantial because claims made by managers, advisors, and consultants are often left unchallenged. This unfortunate state of affairs can be reduced in several ways depending on the circumstances:

- Requesting empirical evidence supporting the skill being marketed by managers, advisors, and forecasters.

In the end, when an organization considers hiring an expert who claims to have a specific forecasting ability, it should request empirical evidence over a long period before arriving at a decision and consider the sample size and the inaccurate as well as the accurate forecasts. Forecasting a recession that does not occur can be costlier (financially and professionally) than failing to forecast a recession. In marketing themselves, forecasters will emphasize only their successful forecasts. It may seem obvious, but the work of Phil Tetlock illustrates that experts with no forecasting abilities can still have very long careers.

- Establishing the rules of a pre- and post-mortem ahead of any important decision. When making an important decision, investment or otherwise, Management should attempt to determine potential issues and consequences before they occur and which metrics will be used to measure success after implementation of this decision.[28] The understanding by all that are involved in the decision process that there will be a defined feedback mechanism and that this information will be communicated will downplay overclaiming at the initial stage.[29] Furthermore, it is also important to manage the effect of surprise. It is much easier for Management to understand and communicate internally unfavorable performances in specific circumstances if Management was already aware of the specific circumstances that would trigger an unfavorable outcome.

Consider, for instance, the implementation of a plan by a pension fund to move away from an indexed equity allocation to products that extract specific factors, such as size, value, momentum, and low-beta. Moving away from an indexed allocation creates a tracking error risk not only against the index, but also possibly against the peer group. Even if Management fully understands this aspect, it is doubtful that most of the pension fund participants do. Implementing a true long-term approach for asset management is challenging.

For example, Andrew Ang mentions how the year 2008 erased all the active returns the Norwegian fund had ever accumulated.[30] The public understood the decline in market returns but not in active returns. The issue at hand is communication and education. The public was well informed of market risk but not of factor risks. They never understood that active management could perform so badly across the board under specific circumstances.

The quant meltdown in 2007 gives a proper example of this risk. During the week of August 6, 2007, a significant decline in the performance of strategies linked to risk factors other than the market portfolio occurred in the U.S. stock market. The cause is believed to be a large fund that closed its positions, thereby precipitating the decline of stocks bought and an increase in stocks sold short by similar funds. What is particular is that important losses were experienced in these strategies, whereas the market index was unaffected. For example, the momentum and low-beta factors ended the week about 3 percent down, while the market was up by more than 1 percent.

We also reported in chapter 6 that on a rolling ten-year basis, 2015 is one of only two periods since the early 1950s in which the market factor dominated all other risk factors. In the first seven months of 2015, the stock market performance was dominated by large market capitalization and growth firms, leaving well behind lower market capitalization and value firms that are the backbone of many smart beta strategies. Amazon alone explained one-third of the rise of the entire consumer discretionary group during this period.[31]

By definition, a risk factor is exposed to bad times. Hence although factor-based products tend to outperform traditional indices in the long run, Management must understand that they can underperform for several years. The most important aspect is to educate Management about the sensitivity of returns to risk factors and how specific products load on these factors. We must do more than manage overclaiming (i.e., that a new strategy will necessarily outperform), we must also manage overexpectations. The following section examines this recommendation further.

Raising the Bar on Benchmarking

Without proper benchmarks, we cannot easily detect or challenge overclaiming. In our industry, significant bonuses and fees are paid, while many researchers have shown the average manager of mutual funds, hedge funds, and private equity has added no value to, and even subtracted value from, fair benchmarks.

When building portfolios in chapter 6, we noted that our framework should also be used to build better benchmarks. We used our return equation to evaluate the merits of three different indices: the RAFI U.S. 1000 Index, the S&P Equal Weight Index, and the Max Diversification USA Index. We put the return of these indices on the left-hand side of our return equation, and market, size, value, and momentum as factors on the right-hand side:

$$R_{product} = R_f + \alpha + \beta_{market}F_{market} + \beta_{size}F_{size} + \beta_{value}F_{value} + \beta_{momentum}F_{momentum} + \varepsilon.$$

Of course, factors can and should vary depending on the product being evaluated. Management should run such regressions and evaluate the product accordingly. For instance, they can prefer their active managers to have low exposures β_{market} and β_{size} to the market and size factors, but high exposures β_{value} and $\beta_{momentum}$ to the value and momentum factors.

The idea is to better assess a manager's worth. Use of multi-factor-based benchmarks helps explain investment performance and better segregate excess performances due to α and exposure to risk factors. A fund manager can add value by outperforming a set of risk factors, that is, by having a high estimated α. He can also add value by appropriately timing his exposures to the different risk factors. Thus, even if managers do not report their performance to Management using a multifactor approach,

Management should request the data that would allow for this analysis. Again, although a positive α is preferable, an investor can be satisfied to achieve a balanced exposure of risk factors at a reasonable cost unless it does not want to expose itself to some of these factors.

It is unusual for managers to use multifactor benchmarks, at least in their reporting to Management. First, it adds an element of complexity to the client reporting, but it also demystifies some of the reported sources of excess performance. Many traditional managers would be uncomfortable with this "transparency." For example, we witnessed the case of an institutional manager using a combination of cash and equity to benchmark their value strategy. The rationale was that as the tilt toward value stock lowered the volatility of the portfolio, a proper benchmark was a watered-down market portfolio, say 85 percent allocated to the market portfolio and 15 percent allocated to cash. This is a badly designed benchmark for two reasons. First, weighting the market portfolio in the benchmark is not necessary. Running this regression will automatically assess the level of market risk in the portfolio through the estimated β_{market}. Second, the value risk factor needs to be included in the analysis, otherwise the value tilt will be misconstrued as α. We are interested in assessing whether the proposed value strategy is good at combining the market and value risk factors, is good at picking particular stocks that will outperform these two factors, or both. Using an 85/15 benchmark is like using a misspecified return equation and assuming arbitrary values for the factor exposures.

The following are examples of potential factors that could be used to design benchmarks such as:

- Private equity: Market (Equity) + Market (Bonds) + Liquidity + Credit
- Corporate bonds: Market (Bonds) + Credit
- Value equity: Market (Equity) + Value

It is unlikely that most managers would use a multifactor-based approach to report their own performance unless it is specifically requested. A first step is for Management to perform their own internal analysis and implement it among managers. It would certainly change the nature of the discussion between managers and Management and help reduce the issues of overclaiming and agency.

Learning to Be More Patient

Sir John Templeton said, "It is impossible to produce a superior performance unless you do something different from the majority." However, it may take much longer than investors expect to increase the likelihood of outperforming an index or specific target. A three-year track record is far from sufficient to judge managerial expertise.

There are also other implications. Management tends to fire a manager after a few years of underperformance. Assuming we truly understand the investment process of the manager and are comfortable holding the strategy on a long-term basis, we should be more concerned with the performance of our portfolio of managers than with the performance of any single manager. In a study of U.S. equity managers done by a consulting firm, 90 percent of top-quartile managers over a ten-year period encountered at least one thirty-six-month period of underperformance. For 50 percent of them, it was five years.[32] Therefore it would be impossible to maintain a long-term investment philosophy if we question the relevance of owning each manager that underperforms for a few years. Firing managers that underperform for a few years without consideration for other factors is akin to not properly rebalancing a portfolio or to buying high and selling low. Retail investors underperform because they buy into rising markets and sell into declining markets. Most of them do not have a process to manage their emotions. It is difficult to maintain a smart long-term invest-ment approach without a proper understanding of the investment process of our managers.

In a 2014 interview, Seth Alexander, Joel Cohen, and Nate Chesley of MIT Investment Management company talk about their process for partnering with investment managers for what they hope will be several decades and how this can be achieved.[33] They make three statements that should resonate with our discussions in this book. First, great investors are focused more on process than outcomes. Of course, the intent is still to outperform in the long run, but they do understand that even the best managers and the best processes can have a mediocre year and three to four years of underperformance. Second, great managers do not have a cookie-cutter approach to investing or try to cater to what they think allocators want; they spend time tailoring their investment approach to what works for them. Hence both great investors and managers must have convictions in the processes. Finally, they state Jeff Bezos who often mentions how if your investment horizon is three years, you are competing against a whole lot of people, but if your time frame is longer, there is a world of other possibilities. Only with a long-term horizon and patience can we truly start emphasizing the importance of process.

Raising the Level of Knowledge in Our Industry

There is a wedge between the state of knowledge in academia and industry practices in the asset management industry. Consider two of the most important developments in the financial litera-ture over the last seventy years: portfolio diversification by Harry Markowitz in 1952 and the capital asset pricing model (CAPM) by William Sharpe in 1964.

The first paper allowed us to understand that portfolio volatil-ity can be reduced for a given level of expected return through diversification, hence increasing compounded returns. The second showed us why risk should be divided between its systematic component (the market), which is compensated by a market risk premium and a nonsystematic component that is unrewarded because it is diversifiable.

Many people dismiss these contributions in the industry. Mean variance investing as described in the first paper is plagued with estimation issues, and naïve implementation is a sure way to lose money. The one-factor CAPM has a poor empirical record as there are other risk factors that are remunerated.

But these papers are practically relevant, and their insights are crucial in a conversation on investments. The difficulties in measuring expected returns, volatilities, and correlations that make the Markowitz portfolios hard to implement in real life can be addressed with different solutions, as we discussed in chapter 6. But most importantly, its insight that diversification is the only free lunch in finance is crucial and underpins many existing investment solutions.

The CAPM is derived using a set of assumptions that are not entirely realistic. Similar to the case of Markowitz's work, subsequent work relaxes these assumptions and provides better performing asset pricing models. But most importantly, the model shows each investor allocating their portfolio results in a risk factor being remunerated with positive expected return and other risks not being remunerated. Extensions of this paper similarly show the economic underpinning for other risk factors to be remunerated in financial markets. This insight allows us to understand that some factors will be remunerated and other types of risk will not.

These insights are crucial in examining the worthiness of new products. What is their source of performance? Are they properly diversified? What are the investors' preferences and market structure that lead to this source of performance being compensated with positive returns?

Even though these papers are several decades old, their insights are often misunderstood, and we are still limited in our ability to explain simple concepts and use standard terminologies when explaining investment strategies to many investors. Continuous and relevant education is essential. Without it, we will keep repeating the same mistakes, rediscovering old investment concepts through different forms, and making investment decisions based on imperfect information. The responsibility should not rest solely on asset managers to better communicate their strategies and know-how, but also on Management to improve their general knowledge of subject matter. We hope that this book has contributed to this end.

Concluding Remarks

It is said that investing is an art and a science. The science part concerns an understanding of performance drivers and methodologies. We live in a multifactor world that requires us to identify what is relevant, what is not, and how to integrate relevant factors. We must also convince investors and their agents of the validity of our approach, and therein lies the "art."

Many investors remain unconvinced of factor-based approaches. We often hear investors say that factor tilt portfolios have considerable risk relative to market capitalization–weighted portfolios. They have underperformed over many periods and entail greater transaction costs.

However, this reasoning is based on the assumption that we live in a single-factor world and that the market factor is always the appropriate benchmark for each of us. It also assumes that the market is the most return/risk efficient portfolio for any investor. However, which is more likely: that we live in a single-factor world or that we live in a multifactor world? That a combination of the market factor and some other riskless asset leads to the most efficient allocation for all of us or that specific combinations of factors could lead to more efficient and appropriate portfolios for some of us?

The key to making good decisions involves "understanding information, integrating information in an internally consistent manner, identifying the relevance of information in a decision process, and inhibiting impulsive responding."[34] When luck plays a small role, a good process will lead to a good outcome. But when luck plays a large role, as in the investment management industry, good outcomes are difficult to predict, a poor state of affairs when patience is in short supply. This book is entirely about the process of making good investment decisions in the long term for patient investors. Implementing a good investment process requires a body of knowledge. Unfortunately, this knowledge may be tainted by biases and conflicts of interests in our industry. Even if we understood the requirements of efficient processes, there are significant implementation challenges. We hope this book provides a step in the right direction and contributes to a productive conversation on investment.

Notes

1. The Subtleties of Asset Management

1. J. Grantham, "Silver Linings and Lessons Learned," *GMO Quarterly Letter* (2008).

2. L. H. Pedersen, *Efficiently Inefficient: How Smart Money Invests and Market Prices Are Determined* (Princeton, NJ: Princeton University Press, 2015).

3. D. Kahneman, *Thinking, Fast and Slow* (New York: Farrar, Straus and Giroux, 2011), 177.

2. Understanding the Playing Field

1. The terms specified in the example are inspired by products sold in Canada. Products sold in the United States have different terms, which are often more favorable than in Canada. For example, in Canada the guaranteed bonus of the benefit base is usually linear (such as 5 percent × 10 years = 50 percent), while in the United States, it is usually compounded ($1.05^{10} - 1 = $ 62.9 percent).

2. A. Ang, *Asset Management: A Systematic Approach to Factor Investing* (Oxford: Oxford University Press, 2014).

3. See, for example, S. J. Grossman and J. E. Stiglitz, "On the Impossibility of Informationally Efficient Markets," *American Economic Review* 70 (1980): 393–408.

4. Investment Company Institute, *2013 Investment Company Fact Book: A Review of Trends and Activity in the U.S. Investment Company Industry*, 53rd edition (2013).

5. E. F. Fama and K. R. French, "Luck Versus Skill in the Cross-Section of Mutual Fund Returns," *Journal of Finance* 65 (2010): 1915–47.

6. J. A. Busse, A. Goyal, and S. Wahal, "Performance and Persistence in Institutional Investment Management," *Journal of Finance* 65 (2010): 765–90.

7. J. A. Busse, A. Goyal, and S. Wahal, "Investing in a Global World," *Review of Finance* 18 (2014): 561–90.

8. Investment Company Institute, *2013 Investment Company Fact Book: A Review of Trends and Activity in the U.S. Investment Company Industry*, 53rd edition (2013).

9. SPIVA U.S. Scorecard, Year-End 2014.

10. D. diBartolomeo and E. Witkowski, "Mutual Fund Misclassification: Evidence Based on Style Analysis," *Financial Analysts Journal* 53 (1997): 32–43; M. Kim, R. Shukla, and M. Tomas, "Mutual Fund Objective Misclassification," *Journal of Economic and Business* 52 (2000): 309–23.

11. J. Lussier and S. Monciaud, "Developing and Investment Culture," Desjardins Global Asset Management (2007).

3. Skill, Scale, and Luck in Active Fund Management

1. M. J. Mauboussin, *The Success Equation: Untangling Skill and Luck in Business, Sports and Investing* (Boston: Harvard Business Review Press, 2012).

2. Ibid.

3. R. C. Grinold, "The Fundamental Law of Active Management," *Journal of Portfolio Management* 15 (1989): 30–37.

4. We simulate the monthly market returns from a normal distribution with annual mean of 5 percent and volatility of 20 percent. We simulate monthly returns of 100,000 funds with a 2 percent alpha, a 5 percent tracking error, and a beta normally distributed around one with volatility 0.2. Funds' idiosyncratic risk is also normally distributed.

5. R. Kosowski, A. Timmermann, R. Wermers, and H. White, "Can Mutual Fund Stars Really Pick Stocks? New Evidence from a Bootstrap Analysis," *Journal of Finance* 61 (2006): 2551–96.

6. L. Barras, O. Scaillet, and R. Wermers, "False Discoveries in Mutual Fund Performance: Measuring Luck in Estimated Alphas," *Journal of Finance* 65 (2010): 179–216.

7. L. Pastor, R. F. Stambaugh, and L. A. Taylor, "Scale and Skill in Active Management," *Journal of Financial Economics* 116 (2015): 23–45.

8. J. B. Berk and J. H. van Binsbergern, "Measuring Skill in the Mutual Fund Industry," *Journal of Financial Economics* 118 (2015): 1–20.

9. See, for example, L. Barras, O. Scaillet, and R. Wermers, "False Discoveries in Mutual Fund Performance: Measuring Luck in Estimated Alphas," *Journal of Finance* 65 (2010): 179–216, and Kosowski, Timmermann, Wermers, and White, "Can Mutual Funds Stars Really Pick Stocks?"

10. M. Kacperczyk, S. Van Nieuwerburgh, and L. Veldkamp, "Time-Varying Fund Manager Skill," *Journal of Finance* 69 (2014): 1455–84.

11. K. J. M. Cremers and A. Petajisto, "How Active Is Your Fund Manager? A New Measure that Predicts Performance," *Review of Financial Studies* 22 (2009): 3329–65.

12. A. Frazzini, J. Friedman, and L. Pomorski, "Deactivating Active Share" (AQR Capital Management white paper, 2015).

13. H. Doshi, R. Elkamhi, and M. Simutin, "Managerial Activeness and Mutual Fund Performance," Forthcoming in *The Review of Asset Pricing Studies* (2016).

14. For an excellent and useful survey, see R. C. Jones and R. Wermers, "Active Management in Mostly Efficient Markets," *Financial Analyst Journal* 67 (2011): 29–45.

15. L. Pastor and R. F. Stambaugh, "On the Size of the Active Management Industry," *Journal of Political Economy* 120 (2012): 740–81.

16. C. D. Ellis, "Murder on the Orient Express: The Mystery of Underperformance," *Financial Analysts Journal* 68 (2012): 13–19.

17. J. C. Bogle, "The Clash of Cultures," *Journal of Portfolio Management* 37 (2011): 14–28.

4. What May and Can Be Forecasted?

1. N. N. Taleb, 2014, *Antifragile: Things That Gain from Disorder* (New York: Random House, 2014), 348.

2. P. E. Tetlock, *Expert Political Judgment: How Good Is It? How Can We Know?* (Princeton, NJ: Princeton University Press, 2006).

3. N. Silver, *The Signal and the Noise: Why So Many Predictions Fail But Some Don't* (New York: Penguin, 2012), 49.

4. Survey of Professional Forecasters, November 13, 2007, Federal Reserve Bank of Philadelphia.

5. Wall Street Economists Institute, Economics Prediction Research Project.

6. Fox News Debate, December 16, 2006, and August 8, 2007.

7. R. Greszler and R. Boccia, *Social Security Trustees Report: Unfunded Liabilities of $1.1 Trillion and Projected Insolvency in 2033* (Washington, DC: Heritage Foundation, 2014).

8. Bloomberg News, March 26, 2009.

9. Bloomberg Television, August 31, 2011.

10. Tweet from Nouriel Roubini, September 2011.

11. Nouriel Roubini, "The Global Stock Market Rally Is Over . . . & The Worst Is Yet To Come," Economywatch, 2012.

12. J. Sommer, "An Ugly Forecast that Has Been Right Before," *New York Times*, October 18, 2011.

13. P. Loungani, "The Arcane Art of Predicting Recessions," *Financial Times*, December 18, 2000.

14. I. Ben-David, J. Graham, and C. R. Harvey, "Managerial Miscalibration," *Quarterly Journal of Economics* 128 (2013): 1547–84.

15. M. Glaser, T. Langer, and M. Weber, "True Overconfidence in Interval Estimates: Evidence Based on a New Measure of Miscalibration," *Journal of Behavioral Decision Making* 26 (2013): 405–17.

16. W. P. Dukes, J. Peng, and P. C. English II, "How Do Practitioners Value Common Stock?" *Journal of Investing* 15 (2006): 90–104.

17. J. Montier, *Behavioural Investing: A Practitioner's Guide to Applying Behavioural Finance* (Chichester, England: Wiley Finance, 2007).

18. J. Montier J., *The Little Book of Behavioural Investing: How Not to Be Your Worst Enemy* (Hoboken, NJ: Wiley, 2010).

19. Transcript of Chairman Bernanke's Press Conference, June 19, 2013.

20. B. Appelbaum, "Two Economies in Turmoil for Different Reasons," *New York Times*, June 21, 2013.

21. Monthly Labor Review, Bureau of Labor Statistics, April 2015.

22. M. L. Finucane and C. M. Gullion, "Developing a Tool for Measuring the Decision-Making Competence of Older Adults," *Psychology and Aging* 25 (2010): 271–88.

23. Edge, "How to Win at Forecasting: A Conversation with Philip Tetlock," 2015, edge.org/conversation/how-to-win-at-forecasting.

24. M. J. Mauboussin, *Think Twice: Harnessing the Power of Counterintuition* (Boston: Harvard Business School Publishing, 2012), 46.

25. K. Storchmann, 2011, "Wine Economics: Emergence, Developments, Topics" (American Association of Wine Economists, AAWE Working Paper No. 85).

26. I. Ayres, *Super Crunchers: Why Thinking-by-Numbers Is the New Way to Be Smart* (New York: Bantam Books, 2007).

27. Orley Ashenfelter, David Ashmore, and Robert Lalonde, "Bordeaux Wine Vintage Quality and the Weather," *Chance* 8 (1995): 7–14.

28. F. Prial, "Wine Talk," *New York Times*, May 23, 1990.

29. J. Y. Campbell and J. H. Cochrane, "By Force of Habit: A Consumption-Based Explanation of Aggregate Stock Market Behavior," *Journal of Political Economy* 107 (1999): 205–51.

30. See, for example, R. F. Stambaugh, "Predictive Regressions," *Journal of Financial Economics* 54 (1999): 375–421.

31. A. Goyal and I. Welch, "A Comprehensive Look at the Empirical Performance of Equity Premium Prediction," *Review of Financial Studies* 21 (2008): 1455–508.

32. J. H. Cochrane, "Presidential Address: Discount Rates," *Journal of Finance* 66 (2011): 1047–108.

33. Ibid.

34. D. Rapach and G. Zhou, "Forecasting Stock Returns," *Handbook of Econometric Forecasting* 2A (2013): 327–83.

35. Note that we employ a simple predictive model based on the combination of the following work: M. I. Ferreira and P. Santa-Clara, "Forecasting Stock Market Returns: The Sum of the Parts Is More Than the Whole," *Journal of Financial Economics* 100 (2011): 514–37, and J. Y. Campbell and S. B. Thompson, "Predicting Excess Stock Returns Out of Sample: Can Anything Beat the Historical Average?" *Review of Financial Studies* 21 (2008): 1509–31.

36. Each period, we find the optimal allocation of an investor with logarithmic utility.

37. P. E. Meehl, *Clinical vs. Statistical Prediction: A Theoretical Analysis and a Review of the Evidence* (Minneapolis: University of Minnesota Press, 1954).

38. W. M. Grove, D. H. Zald, A. M. Hallberg, B. Lebow, E. Snitz, and C. Nelson, "Clinical Versus Mechanical Prediction: A Meta-Analysis," *Psychological Assessment* 12 (2000): 19–30.

39. See L. Landro, "The Secret to Fighting Infection," *Wall Street Journal*, March 27 2011, and "Three Years Out, Safety Checklists Keeps Hospital Infections in Check," *Journal of Nursing* 40, (2010): 21–23.

40. W. M. Grove and P. E. Meehl, "Comparative Efficiency of Formal (Mechanical, Algorithmic) and Informal (Subjective, Impressionistic) Prediction Procedures: The Clinical/Statistical Controversy," *Psychology, Public Policy, and the Law* 2 (1997): 293–323.

41. N. N. Taleb, 2014, *Antifragile: Things that Gain from Disorder* (New York: Random House, 2014): 11.

42. We use a NGARCH model on all daily returns available at each point in time to ensure our results are out-of-sample. The monthly volatility predictions are implied by the model estimates and the last filtered conditional volatility.

43. To obtain time-varying volatility, we fit a NGARCH on monthly returns of the S&P 500 and on monthly returns of the portfolio that targets a 10 percent annual volatility.

5. The Blueprint to Long-Term Performance

1. J. Montier, *The Little Book of Behavioural Investing: How Not to Be Your Worst Enemy* (Hoboken, NJ: Wiley, 2010), 70.

2. C. B. Erb and C. R. Harvey, "The Strategic and Tactical Value of Commodity Futures," *Financial Analysts Journal* 62 (2006): 69–97.

3. G. Gorton and G. Rouwenhorst, "Facts and Fantasies About Commodity Futures," *Financial Analysts Journal* 62 (2006): 47–68.

4. We use the fact that the geometric mean of a portfolio with an allocation of ω to one risky asset is given by $R_f + \omega E[R - R_f] - \frac{1}{2} \omega^2 Var[R]$ so $\omega^* = (E[r - R_f] / Var[R])$.

5. We estimate a bivariate GARCH on monthly returns for the S&P 500 Index (from Bloomberg) and the ten-year U.S. government bond (from CRSP) from February 1971 to March 2015. The 60/40 portfolio is rebalanced every month.

6. We use monthly returns for the S&P 500 Index (from Bloomberg) and the ten-year U.S. government bond (from CRSP) from February 1971 to March 2015. The 60/40 portfolio is rebalanced every month. We use the monthly returns of the market, SMB, HML, and UMD factors and the one-month U.S. T-Bill rate of return obtained from Kenneth French's website. The factor exposure is obtained by estimating an AR(1)-NGARCH for each asset to obtain the conditional variances and a dynamic normal copula model to obtain the dynamic correlations.

7. R. S. J. Koijen, H. Lustig, and S. Van Nieuwerburgh, "The Cross-Section and Time-Series of Stock and Bond Returns" (NBER Working paper, New York University, 2015).

8. L. Zhang, "The Value Premium," *Journal of Finance* 60 (2005): 67–103.

9. See, for example, R. Jagannathan and Z. Wang, "The Conditional CAPM and the Cross-Section of Expected Returns," *Journal of Finance* 51 (1996): 3–53, and S. Betermier, L. E. Calvet, and P. Sodini, "Who Are the Value and Growth Investors?" Forthcoming in *The Journal of Finance* (2016).

10. J. Berk, "A Critique of Size-Related Anomalies," *Review of Financial Studies* 8 (1995): 275–86.

11. See A. Perold, "Fundamentally Flawed Indexing," *Financial Analyst Journal* 68 (2007): 31–37.

12. M. J. Brennan and A. W. Wang, "The Mispricing Return Premium," *Review of Financial Studies* 23 (2010): 3437–68.

13. J. H. Cochrane, "Presidential Address: Discount Rates," *Journal of Finance* 66 (2011): 1047–108.

14. C. S. Asness, T. J. Moskowitz, and L. H. Pedersen, "Value and Momentum Everywhere," *Journal of Finance* 68 (2013): 929–85.

15. H. Lustig, N. Roussanov, and A. Verdelhan, "Common Risk Factors in Currency Markets," *Review of Finance Studies* 24 (2011): 3731–77.

16. C. R. Harvey, Y. Liu, and H. Zhu, ". . . and the Cross-Section of Expected Returns" *Review of Financial Studies* 29 (2016): 5–68.

17. D. McLean and J. Pontiff, "Does Academic Research Destroy Stock Return Predictability?" *Journal of Finance* 71 (2016): 5–32.

6. Building Better Portfolios

1. We use the term *factor* somewhat loosely here. Risk factors usually refer to sources of expected returns linked to a rational compensation for risk, not to mispricings. But as we discussed in chapter 5, building a strategy that tries to exploits mispricings is similar to building risk factors. From investors' perspective, as opposed to the academic asset pricers' perspective, the difference is less important.

2. Available on Professor Ken French's website at http://mba.tuck.dartmouth.edu/pages/faculty/ken.french/data_library.html.

3. https://www.aqr.com/library/data-sets.

4. Some time series will unfortunately require the reader to have subscription to data providers such as Bloomberg and Datastream.

5. V. Acharya and L. H. Pedersen, "Asset Pricing with Liquidity Risk," *Journal of Financial Economics* 77 (2005): 375–410.

6. See M. Rubinstein, "The Fundamental Theorem of Parameter-Preference Security Valuation," *Journal of Financial and Quantitative Analysis* 8 (1973): 61–69; A. K. Kraus and R. H. Litzenberger, "Skewness Preference and the Valuation of Risk Assets," *Journal of Finance* 31 (1976): 1085–100; and C. R. Harvey and A. Siddique, "Conditional Skewness in Asset Pricing Tests," *Journal of Finance* 55 (2000): 1263–95.

7. C. Asness and A. Frazzini, "The Devil in HML's Details," *Journal of Portfolio Management* 39 (2013): 49–68.

8. P. Christoffersen and H. Langlois, "The Joint Dynamics of Equity Market Factors," *Journal of Financial and Quantitative Analysis* 48 (2013): 1371–404.

9. J. H. Cochrane, "A Mean-Variance Benchmark for Intertemporal Portfolio Theory," *Journal of Finance* 69 (2014): 1–49.

10. The optimal mean-variance allocation is given by $\omega = \Sigma^{-1}\mu \,/\, \gamma$, where Σ is the covariance matrix of returns, μ is the vector of expected excess returns, and γ is the investor's degree of risk aversion.

11. We use an exponentially weighted average on daily returns with a parameter of 0.94 as in the earlier J. P. Morgan RiskMetrics model.

12. See, for example, R. C. Merton, "On Estimating the Expected Return on the Market," *Journal of Financial Economics* 8 (1980): 323–61.

13. Note here that we use the term *leverage* somewhat loosely to mean the sum of factor weights. As four of these factors involve short positions, and as many positions could cancel out between factors, the gross leverage could actually be different from 200 percent.

14. We use the FTSE RAFI US 1000 Total Return Index (Bloomberg ticker FR10XTR Index) and the S&P 500 Equal Weight Total Return Index (Bloomberg ticker SPXEWTR Index). The FTSE TOBAM MaxDiv USA $ Index was provided by TOBAM. The risk-free rate and all factor returns are from AQR's data library. We use Newey-West standard errors. ** indicates statistical significance at the 1 percent level and * at the 5 percent level.

15. Presentation to the Q-Group Spring 2007 Seminar, "Non-Cap Weighted Indices," available at https://www.aqr.com/~/media/files/perspectives/q-group-presentation-fundamental-investing.pdf?la=en.

16. See R. Kan and G. Zhou, "Optimal Portfolio Choice with Parameter Uncertainty," *Journal of Financial and Quantitative Analysis* 42 (2007): 621–56, and J. Tu and G. Zhou, "Markowitz Meets Talmud: A Combination of Sophisticated and Naïve Diversification Strategies," *Journal of Financial Economics* 99 (2011): 204–15.

17. Y. Choueifaty and Y. Coignard, "Toward Maximum Diversification," *Journal of Portfolio Management* 35 (2008): 40–51.

18. To see this, note that the maximum Sharpe ratio portfolio maximize the ratio $\omega^{T}\mu \,/\, \sqrt{(\omega^{T}\Sigma\omega)}$, where μ is the vector of expected excess returns, ω is the vector of portfolio weights, and Σ is the matrix of covariances. If we assume that expected excess returns are proportional to volatilities, $\mu = K\sigma$, where K is a constant and σ is the vector of volatilities, the ratio becomes $K\omega^{T}\sigma \,/\, \sqrt{(\omega^{T}\Sigma\omega)}$. Because K has no incidence on the maximization, the ratio is the same as the one the maximum diversification portfolio maximizes.

19. Countries in Europe include Austria, Belgium, Switzerland, Germany, Denmark, Spain, Finland, France, United Kingdom, Greece, Ireland, Israel, Italy, Netherlands, Norway, Portugal, and Sweden. North American countries include Canada and the United States. The Pacific region is composed of Australia, Hong Kong, Japan, New Zealand, and Singapore.

20. E. F. Fama and K. R. French, "Size, Value, and Momentum in International Stock Returns," *Journal of Financial Economics* 105 (2012): 457–72.

21. U.S. Treasury fixed term bond indices are available from CRSP for maturities of 1, 2, 5, 7, 10, 20, and 30 years. These test portfolios are strictly speaking not portfolios because a single representative bond is chosen each month. At the end of each month, a representative bond for each maturity is chosen and held for the next month. A representative bond is the most recently issued among all that are fully taxable, noncallable, nonflower, and at least six months from but closest to the maturity date. Flower bonds are considered if no bond meets these criteria. The details for constructing the value-weighted market portfolio of all bonds can be found in H. Langlois, "Asset Pricing with Return Asymmetries: Theory and Tests" (Working paper, HEC Paris, 2014).

22. See, for example, C. R. Harvey, "The Real Term Structure and Consumption Growth," *Journal of Financial Economics* 22 (1988): 305–33.

23. We use the composition of the S&P Goldman Sachs Commodity Index as our sample of commodity futures. This index contains twenty-four traded contracts covering six categories: energy (WTI crude oil, Brent crude oil, RBOB gasoline, heating oil, gas oil, and natural gas), industrial metals (aluminum, copper, lead, nickel, and zinc), precious metals (gold and silver), agriculture: grains and oil seeds (wheat, Kansas wheat, corn, and soybeans), agriculture: softs (cotton, sugar, coffee, and cocoa), and livestock (feeder cattle, live cattle, and lean hogs). We use contracts as they become available. We obtain futures quotes from Bloomberg for all available maturities. For each commodity futures, we construct a time series of total returns by investing each month in the futures contract whose maturity is the nearest maturity coming later than the end of the month.

24. We obtain spot exchange rates and one-month forward rates from Datastream for sixteen countries: Belgium, France, Germany, Italy, the Netherlands (all replaced by the Euro starting in January 1999), Australia, Canada, Denmark, Hong Kong, Japan, New Zealand, Norway, Singapore, Sweden, Switzerland, and the United Kingdom. All rates are expressed in U.S. dollars per unit of foreign currency and are collected by Barclays Bank International. Not all exchange rates are available each month; we have a minimum of seven and a maximum of fifteen over time. The introduction of the Euro is responsible for a decrease in the number of currencies available.

25. Basis is computed as the negative of the logarithm-difference of the futures with a maturity closest to one year ahead and the futures with the closest maturity.

26. The interest rates differential is the one implied by spot and forward rates. We average the daily differentials over the previous month to control for outliers.

27. See F. Yang, "Investment Shocks and the Commodity Basis Spread," *Journal of Financial Economics* 110 (2013): 164–84, and G. Gorton, F. Hayashi, and G. Rouwenhorst, "The Fundamentals of Commodity Futures Returns," *Review of Finance* 17 (2013): 35–105.

28. H. Lustig, N. Roussanov, and A. Verdelhan, "Common Risk Factors in Currency Markets," *Review of Financial Studies* 24 (2011): 3731–77.

29. A. Illmanen and J. Kizer, "The Death of Diversification Has Been Greatly Exaggerated," *Journal of Portfolio Management* 38 (2012): 15–27.

30. M. A. Ferreira and P. Santa-Clara, "Forecasting Stock Market Returns: The Sum of the Parts Is More than the Whole," *Journal of Financial Economics* 100 (2011): 514–37.

31. For each asset, we compute the one month ahead prediction, which is the payout yield scaled to a monthly horizon. Over the longest return history available for each asset, we compute the out-of-sample R^2 as in J. Y. Campbell and S. B. Thompson, "Predicting Excess Stock Returns Out of Sample: Can Anything Beat the Historical Average?" *Review of Financial Studies* 21 (2008): 1509–31. R^2 vary from 1 percent to 11 percent for all equity and bond indices, meaning that the predictions have lower mean squared errors than using the sample average excess return as a prediction.

32. R. Jagannathan and T. Ma, "Risk Reduction in Large Portfolios: Why Imposing the Wrong Constraints Helps," *Journal of Finance* 58 (2003): 1651–83.

33. V. DeMiguel, L. Garlappi, F. J. Nogales, and R. Uppal, "A Generalized Approach to Portfolio Optimization: Improving Performance by Constraining Portfolio Norms," *Management Science* 55 (2009): 798–812.

34. See O. Ledoit and M. Wolf, "Improved Estimation of the Covariance Matrix of Stock Returns with an Application to Portfolio Selection," *Journal of Empirical Finance* 10 (2003): 603–21, and O. Ledoit and M. Wolf, "A Well-Conditioned Estimator for Large-Dimensional Covariance Matrices," *Journal of Multivariate Analysis* 88 (2004): 365–411.

35. We may say here that our rebalancing frequency is exogenously determined by our preferences, not endogenously determined by asset price dynamics.

36. This fact may be due to our current state of knowledge about volatility and correlation modeling. It is entirely possible that as we become better at estimating time-varying volatilities and correlations that nonnormal

features such as fat tails and asymmetries would become less important. This is not the case for the time being.

37. P. Christoffersen and H. Langlois, "The Joint Dynamics of Equity Market Factors," *Journal of Financial and Quantitative Analysis* 48 (2013): 1371–404.

38. See, for example, M. W. Brandt, "Estimating Portfolio and Consumption Choice: A Conditional Euler Equations Approach," *Journal of Finance* 54 (1999): 1609–46; Y. Ait-Sahalia and M. W. Brandt, "Variable Selection for Portfolio Choice," *Journal of Finance* 56 (2001): 1297–351; and M. W. Brandt, P. Santa-Clara, and R. Valkanov, "Parametric Portfolio Policies: Exploiting Characteristics in the Cross Section of Equity Returns," *Review of Financial Studies* 22 (2009): 3411–47.

39. Y. Ait-Sahalia and M. W. Brandt, "Variable Selection for Portfolio Choice," *Journal of Finance* 56 (2001): 1297–351.

40. See, for example, A. Ang, D. Papanikolaou, and M. M. Westerfield, "Portfolio Choice with Illiquid Assets" (Working paper, Columbia Business School, 2014).

41. A. Ang, *Asset Management: A Systematic Approach to Factor Investing* (Oxford: Oxford University Press, 2014).

42. From Datastream, we obtain the one- to three-year Canadian Government Bond Index (ACNGVG1) and the over ten-year Canadian Government Bond Index (TCNGVG5).

43. We compute beta using an exponentially weighted moving average on monthly portfolio and currency returns.

44. C. B. Erb and C. R. Harvey, "The Golden Dilemma," *Financial Analyst Journal* 69 (2013): 10–42.

7. We Know Better, But . . .

1. N. Silver, *The Signal and the Noise* (New York: Penguin, 2012), 324.

2. S. Lack, *The Hedge Fund Mirage: The Illusion of Big Money and Why It's Too Good to Be True* (Hoboken, NJ: Wiley, 2012).

3. C. Ellis, *Winning the Loser's Game: Timeless Strategies for Successful Investing*, 6th ed. (New York: McGraw-Hill, 2013).

4. B. Englich and T. Mussweiler, "Sentencing Under Uncertainty: Anchoring Effects in the Courtroom," *Journal of Applied Social Psychology* 31 (2001): 1535–51.

5. Daniel Kahneman, *Thinking, Fast and Slow* (New York: Farrar, Straus and Giroux, 2011).

6. A. Tversky and D. Kahneman, "Judgment Under Uncertainty: Heuristics and Biases," *Sciences*, n.s. 185 (1974): 1124–31.

7. M. G. Haselton, D. Nettle, and P. W. Andrews, "The Evolution of Cognitive Biases," in *The Handbook of Evolutionary Psychology*, ed. D. M. Buss (Hoboken, NJ: Wiley, 2005), 724–46.

8. J. Montier, *The Little Book of Behavioural Investing: How Not to Be Your Own Worst Enemy* (Hoboken, NJ: Wiley, 2010), 6.

9. Investment Innovation Conference, Scottsdale, November 6–8, 2013.

10. J. Montier, *Behavioural Investing: A Practitioners Guide to Applying Behavioural Finance* (Chichester, England: Wiley Finance, 2007), 129.

11. C. M. Reinhart and V. R. Reinhart, "After the Fall" (NBER Working Paper No. 16334, 2010).

12. M. G. Haselton, D. Nettle, and P. W. Andrews, "The Evolution of Cognitive Biases," in *The Handbook of Evolutionary Psychology*, ed. David M. Buss (Hoboken, NJ: Wiley, 2005), 724–746.

13. C. MacKay, *Extraordinary Popular Delusions and the Madness of Crowds (with a foreword by Andrew Tobias, 1841)* (New York: Harmony Books, 1980).

14. Z. Kunda, "The Case for Motivated Reasoning," *Psychological Bulletin* 108 (1990): 480–98.

15. R. Nickerson, "Confirmation Bias: A Ubiquitous Phenomenon on Many Guises," *Review of General Psychology* 2, no. 2 (2009): 175–220.

16. Based on citations reported on Google Scholar.

17. B. Gaylord, "Nate Silver's Model vs. The Morris Law," TownHall.com, 2012.

18. A. Khorona, H. Sarvaes, and P. Tufano, "Mutual Fund Fees Around the World," *Review of Financial Studies* 21 (2009): 2379–416.

19. http://www.bnn.ca/News/2014/11/5/Trailing-fees-What-your-mutual-fund-advisor-now-has-to-tell-you.aspx.

20. Investor Economics and Strategic Insight, *Monitoring Trends in Mutual Fund Cost of Ownership and Expense Ratios: A Canada–U.S. Perspective* (Toronto: Investment Funds Institute of Canada, 2012).

21. H. R. Arkes, R. M. Dawes, and C. Christensen, "Factors Influencing the Use of a Decision Rule in a Probabilistic Task," *Organizational Behavior and Human Decision Processes* 37 (1986): 93–110.

22. Michael J. Mauboussin, *Think Twice: Harnessing the Power of Counterintuition* (Boston: Harvard Business Press, 2012), 33.

23. R. Briner, D. Denyer, and D. M. Rousseau, "Evidence-Based Management: Concept Clean-Up Time?" *Academy of Management Perspectives* 23 (2009): 5–18.

24. J. Pfeffer and R. I. Sutton, *Management Half-Truths and Nonsense: How to Practice Evidence-Based Management, Adapted from Hard Facts, Dangerous Half-Truths, and Total Nonsense: Profiting from Evidence-Based Management* (Cambridge: Harvard Business School Press, 2006).

25. H. Berman, *Making a Difference: The Management and Governance of Non-Profit Enterprises* (Rochester: Rochester Institute of Technology, 2010).

26. S. Efron and R. Gerlsbeck, "MoneySense Answers Your 20 Burning RRSP Questions," *Maclean's*, February 9, 2015. http://www.macleans.ca /economy/money-economy/moneysense-answers-20-burning-rrsp-questions/.

27. For an excellent overview of the literature on liquidity risk, we refer the reader to Y. Amihud, H. Mendelson, and L. H. Pedersen, *Market Liquidity: Asset Pricing, Risk, and Crises* (Cambridge: Cambridge University Press, 2013), and T. Foucault, M. Pagano, and A. Röell, *Market Liquidity: Theory, Evidence, and Policy* (Oxford: Oxford University Press, 2013).

28. G. Klein, "Performing a Project Premortem," *Harvard Business Review* 85 (2007): 18–19.

29. K. Savitsky, L. Van Boven, N. Epley, and W. Wight, "The Unpacking Effect in Responsibility Allocations for Group Tasks," *Journal of Experimental Social Psychology* 41 (2005): 447–57.

30. A. Ang, *Asset Management: A Systematic Approach to Factor Investing* (Oxford: Oxford University Press, 2014).

31. J. Ciolli, "Dumb Beta Strikes Back for U.S. Stocks Starved of Breadth," *Bloomberg News*, August 4, 2015.

32. M. Rice and G. Strotman, *The Next Chapter in the Active vs. Passive Management Debate* (Chicago: DiMeo Schneider and Associates, LLC Research and Associates, 2007).

33. "Manual of Ideas, MITIMCo: Perspectives for Aspiring Superinvestors, Exclusive interview with Seth Alexander, Johel Cohen, and Nate Chesly," MIT Investment Management Company, December 2014.

34. M. L. Finucane and C. M. Gullion, "Developing a Tool for Measuring the Decision-Making Competence of Older Adults," *Psychology and Aging* 25 (2010): 271–88.

Index

price-to-book value, 105
Princeton University, 76, 160
prior probabilities, 175
private equity, 201
professional forecasters: accuracy
  of, 62–63, 73–74; bad
  predictions by, 63; predictions
  by, 60; two groups of, 64
professional fund manager, 8
Pronovost, Peter, 81
PSP. *See* performance-seeking
  portfolios
psychology, 182
publicly traded asset classes, 140

quant meltdown, 124, 199

RAFI. *See* Research Affiliates'
  Fundamental Indexes
RAFI U.S. 1000 Index, 200
*Random Walk Down Wall Street,
  A* (Malkiel), 76
rank-based factors, 119
Rapach, David, 78
rationality: limits of, 170–81;
  requirements of, 190–205
Real Return Bonds, 164
rebalancing frequency, 157, 216n35
recessions: forecasting of, 65; onset
  of, 102
regression to the mean, 42, 177
Reinhart, Carmen and Vincent, 181
Research Affiliates' Fundamental
  Indexes (RAFI), 109, 110, 134;
  RAFI U.S. 1000 Index, 200
retail investors: benchmarks for,
  149; underperformance by, 202
return differential, 132
return equation, 42; average returns
  from, 88; for benchmarks, 200;
  cash flows in, 105; diversification

in, 113; explanation of, 23–25;
  on market portfolio, 26
returns: factors in, 96–97;
  predictability of, 76, 80, 113
Review of Financial Studies, 76,
  138
risk-adjusted returns, 43
risk factors: allocation to, 146;
  Ang, 98–99; diversification of,
  93, 116, 145, 146; exposure to,
  42, 44, 100, 110, 201; factors
  of, 99; fishing for, 112; historical
  performance of, 143; importance
  of, 93; loose usage of, 213n1;
  measurement of, 88; prediction
  of, 82; spikes in, 84; systematic
  sources of, 23, 107; traditional
  portfolio exposure to, 97, 98; of
  U.S. equity, 130
risk management, 37, 38
risk model: estimation of, 159;
  with mean reversion, 155;
  sophistication of, 156
risk premium, 110
risks, 11; active position on, 26;
  adversity to, 20; allocation of,
  126; balance of, 102; sources of,
  89, 96–103
Roubini, Nouriel, 62, 63
Russell 1000 Value Indices, 44

Saint-Louis University, 78
sample size: forecasting affected by,
  64; lack of attention on, 175;
  role in determining investing skill
  of, 39
Santa-Clara, Pedro, 149
Scaillet, Olivier, 47
Schiff, Peter, 62, 63
scientific method, 82
SEC, 56